A Life of Miracles

My Supernatural Journey

Dr. Holly L. Noe

ENDORSEMENTS

Dr. Holly L. Noe's new book "A Life of Miracles, My Supernatural Journey" is very anointed and contains a powerful message to the church. Even as we worked on it as a publishing team we sensed the presence of the Lord manifesting from the pages. I personally look forward to diving in again and again to this incredible story of a remarkable woman who has made such an impact on so many lives around the world. I sense the Holy Spirit will really use this book as a teaching tool on the anointing and living a life of miracles.

"A Life of Miracles" will be read many times even when dear Holly graduates to heaven... a lasting legacy indeed. It was a real honor to work on this project and I pray Dr. Holly will continue to write books for she has much yet to give Christ's Bride

Steve Porter
Deeper Life Press- Publisher
Refuge Ministries

Dr. Holly L. Noe is a mighty servant of God. She ministers in the Gifts of healing and deliverance. Dr. Holly L. Noe has traveled as a missionary to Guatemala spreading the Good News of Jesus Christ with signs following. Her personality and the gift to talk to anyone has allowed her to not only minister in large gatherings, but small gatherings as well. Rev. Noe has the ability to reach out to the local people. She was willing to go out on the streets of Guatemala and to villages to minister to the people. I have had the pleasure of listening to her minister in our church and was captivated by her knowledge in the missionary field.

Chancellor Dr. Paul J. Forti
Grace Christian College and Theological Seminary
Loris, South Carolina

In the pages of this book A Life Of Miracles, My Supernatural Journey, you will feel the passion our dear Rev. Holly Noe writes about in such a way, it jumps off the page and will grip your heart.

I had the opportunity to meet Rev. Holly Noe unexpectedly, however under the leading of God. She is an enterprising woman, without limitations investing in the establishment of the Kingdom of God in Guatemala. When I met her, it did not take much to perceive her passion for the work of God and for our beloved Guatemala and most of all her love for the Presence of God. Today she prepares for one of her most exciting missionary adventures in favor of one of the most challenging projects of her life THE JOSHUA PROJECT.

From Chamelco To The City

For years Dr. Holly Noe sowed not only her life and time in the community of Chamelco, department of Cobán Guatemala but also sowed her personal resources and donations from people who believe in her great vision. After many years of working in this mountainous region of Guatemala, God began to speak to her about the southern part of Guatemala City... Obedient to this divine impulse the Lord reveals the place and the congregation to where she should channel her missionary efforts, the Church where I pastor, Christ Loves You. This congregation initiated a project that had been named JOSHUA, which from its beginnings presented challenges that far surpassed the congregation, nevertheless they relied on the intervention of God, and so it was, the answer was given when God providentially sent a woman passionate about the Kingdom and Guatemala, and Revival, The Missionary Holly Noe.

Adoption of Joshua Project

One visit was enough for Holly to be convinced of the project to which God was mobilizing her to continue her missionary work. On her first visit Dr. Holly declared a word that produced faith in the heart of the church and their pastors. Pastors Hector and Betzy were surprised by that word which promised that God would not only fulfill their dreams for that project but that those dreams would be surpassed beyond their greatest expectations

Thus, begins a vision that has not stopped.

Beginning of Project

Dr. Holly Noe tours congregations raising funds in the United States, full of faith, love, fire and passion. The endorsement of God did not tarry and the construction begins on the TEMPLE JOSHUA. After several visits with her teams Holly begins to plant the first seeds sent to the project, her project. Filled with joy and before the eyes of the whole congregation she begins to raise a temple for 800 people and classrooms for children.

A Story That Does Not End

Rev. Holly L. Noe prepares for more missionary trips, Guatemala is her destiny, no one stops her, she is unstoppable, she walks with God and will not rest until the Joshua project is finished, the project where God continues His glorious work. All the glory is for Him.

Pastors Barillas-Monroy
Christ Loves You Church
Petapa, Villa Hermosa, Guatemala
Presbyter AG Guatemala

I opened the document to edit without any preconceived notions or opinion. However, since the book came to me having been translated from English I was somewhat curious. I couldn't imagine how much it would make me laugh but also, how much it would make me cry. In addition, it provoked me to confront myself regarding the little or nothing I do, having the capacity to see, hear, speak and to walk.

The author draws a picture with her very pleasing personality. Reviewing her writing, one would think how difficult it is to reach such spirituality. Dr. Holly L. Noe writes with an urgency and a burning desire detailing the urgency she feels for the church to seek a fresh encounter with the Holy Spirit. In her narration, she gives the reader an assurance that allows her readers to also feel the Presence of the Lord. This book recounts a powerful testimony and invites people to be involved in missions.

The investigation, communication, and planning are interwoven tools supporting someone who is clear on their mission. Throughout these pages, Dr. Holly clearly narrates the what, how, and where she completes her assignment being surrendered to the perfect will of God who sustains her. There are not many that allow themselves to be so vulnerable in presenting their vision allowing for such public scrutiny and portraying their reasonable, desired objective. To do so is a decision of people of faith who have conviction of their calling.

Immense credit goes to Dr. Holly L. Noe in detailing the accomplishments that have been made possible through her great love for God's work and reproducing her vision in others to the benefit of all who have received from her ministry.

This book will revitalize your belief for the need of missions. It is a realistic account of her work, executed through her teams that go with her. There are very few that reach out and relate to the spiritual and physical needs of this world and feel such an intense love to meet the needs of others.

Finally, Dr. Holly L. Noe teaches us that is possible to give, to teach, instruct, and to participate putting into practice in a responsible manner with an absolute surrender the doctrine that Jesus Christ has taught us and commissioned us to take to the ends of the earth.

Sadie Hernandez

Director International and Interdenominational Magazine

Assemblies of God

Subete Aca (Come up Here)

FORWARD

I have known Holly Noe for over 30 years. I have known her as a missionary, as a preacher and someone who has a miraculous testimony. It is not easy to give a short summary about this outstanding servant of God. However, I would like to say that she has died to self in order to teach ministers that the only way a person can light the flame of Revival is precisely dying to self.

She has always been faithful with the people God has placed at her side to accomplish the work he has given her. Her 48 years of ministry and 20 years as Missionary to Guatemala are a demonstration of her faithfulness to God. Among the works she has accomplished are: missions, churches, and an elementary school. She is an excellent mentor.

Her own life is a miracle. God has kept her in spite of her pain and suffering to glorify Himself in her. Her physical condition having needles embedded in sensitive parts of her body have served to bring people as they see the miracles and believe. Her battle for deliverance from demonic powers and her victories are her testimonies that impact all those who also have addictions and are possessed so that they can see they too can overcome.

This book is a blessing because of her experiences but overall her testimony will win many more. God enabled her to earn her Doctorate in Theology so that she has a deeper knowledge of the Word of God. These pages reflect a high academic preparation, which does not obscure her immense sensitivity and the permanent Presence of the Holy Spirit in her ministerial and personal life.

I have observed her from my youth the way she has gone through many trials and sufferings and yet brought out in her ministry many teachings she learned from all she's gone through. Concerning my admiration for her ministry, I should summarize my testimony of her faithfulness to the Assembly of God. I was very young when I met her; I have since filled many diverse roles excelling to my present position as Superintendent, and Holly has been there at all times and has been faithful and constant.

Having observed her closely, I firmly believe God has backed her and preserved her life for such a time as this; so that we can see that God is faithful with those who renounce "self" and give themselves to His Call.

It's in times like these, we need ministers with the conviction of Dr. Holly L. Noe. We need in times we're living in to edify ourselves with the testimonies like those that are written in the pages of this book.

Rev. Manuel Álvarez
Superintendent Spanish Eastern District
Assemblies of God

ACKNOWLEDGEMENTS

Thank you to my Wonderful, magnificent, Awesome Lord who enabled and anointed me to write. The Holy Spirit truly birthed a gift in me in the writing of my autobiography, and to Him be all the glory.

Fondest memories and thankfulness for my mentor and spiritual mother Nancy Stein who labored sacrificially to pour into my life the Word of God that transformed me.

Blessings to my wonderful and dedicated associate and best friend Lois for helping in proofreading and gathering my thoughts and recalling the many experiences we went through together on the mission field and in the many countries we traveled together through 30 years of ministry. Thanks, for all your encouragement and confidence that enabled me to keep on writing even in difficult times. You truly helped me carry the burden.

Thank you, Heidi Baker for your Word from God. "Guatemala is bigger than you think." It has been confirmed over and over again.

My deepest appreciation for Pastor Kilpatrick, Steve Hill, Lindell Cooley, and Dr. Michael Brown for impartation and your leadership in the Pensacola Outpouring. Thank you for being Presence oriented and not Program oriented. You gave me reason to write about Revival. It changed my life and ministry and has birthed in me a passion for His Presence and imparting it to others.

I would like to express my gratitude to the many people who saw me through this book; to all those who provided support, talked things over, read, wrote, offered comments, and assisted in the editing, proofreading and design. Special thanks to Ken Darrow for Editing English version and Jason Cantrox for Spanish translation.

Thank you to Rev. Manny Alvarez my District Superintendent, of our Spanish Eastern District for his love and support and for believing in me.

Special recognition and thanks to Sadie Hernandez, Director of the International magazine SUBETE ACA. You did an amazing job editing the Spanish version of book. You were a tremendous encouragement to me during the writing process.

To the many pastors and colleagues that assured me they were anxiously waiting for the completion of the book so they could read it. You propelled me to the finish line.

My sincere appreciation for the several days Tom Waddington invested in helping me do a preliminary outline which was my main structure of the book.

Thank you to Steve Porter, my Publisher for encouraging me to write because you recognized God had gifted me. Thank you for your patience with all the questions and need for orientation on the publishing process. I promise the next books will be easier on you. You are truly anointed in what you do not only as a Publisher but as a minister of the Word of God. Thank you for your vision to make it possible for ministers, missionaries and pastors to publish their books.

Thank you to Nereida Esquilin for translating additions made at the midnight hour. Her contribution was invaluable to the success of this project and her friendship much appreciated as always.

TABLE OF CONTENTS

Psalm 116: My Song Of Deliverance

1. I love the Lord, because he hath heard my voice and my supplications.

2. Because he hath inclined his ear unto me, therefore will I call upon him as long as I live.

3. The sorrows of death compassed me, and the pains of hell gat hold upon me: I found trouble and sorrow.

4. Then called I upon the name of the Lord; O Lord, I beseech thee, deliver my soul.

5. Gracious is the Lord, and righteous; yea, our God is merciful.

6. The Lord preserveth the simple: I was brought low, and he helped me.

7. Return unto thy rest, O my soul; for the Lord hath dealt bountifully with thee.

8. For thou hast delivered my soul from death, mine eyes from tears, and my feet from falling.

9. I will walk before the Lord in the land of the living.

10. *I believed, therefore have I spoken: I was greatly afflicted:*

11. *I said in my haste, All men are liars.*

12. *What shall I render unto the Lord for all his benefits toward me?*

13. *I will take the cup of salvation, and call upon the name of the Lord.*

14. *I will pay my vows unto the Lord now in the presence of all his people15 Precious in the sight of the Lord is the death of his saints.*

15. *O Lord, truly I am thy servant; I am thy servant, and the son of thine handmaid: thou hast loosed my bonds.*

16. *I will offer to thee the sacrifice of thanksgiving, and will call upon the name of the Lord.*

17. *I will pay my vows unto the Lord now in the presence of all his people.*

18. *In the courts of the Lord's house, in the midst of thee, O Jerusalem. Praise ye the Lord.*

PART 1

SALVATION AND DELIVERANCE

LOOK WHAT THE LORD HAS DONE; HE SAVED ME JUST IN TIME!

CHAPTER 1

THE BEGINNING OF SORROWS

I love the Lord, because He has heard my voice and my supplication.
Psalms 116:1

For me to live is Christ and to die is gain.
Philippians 1:21

Everything had come to a screeching halt in my life and I had come to the end of a DEAD END street. Every avenue had been traveled and every medical and psychological possibility had been explored and the prognosis was, "NO HOPE, NOTHING CAN STOP HER. LOCK HER UP AND WAIT FOR HER TO KNOCK HER HEAD AGAINST THE WALL AND KILL HERSELF."

BUT GOD HAD A DIFFERENT IDEA. That's why I can truly say, "I love the Lord with all of my heart and soul and strength," and, "FOR ME TO LIVE IS CHRIST." It is an understatement to say I am alive by a miracle of God's saving grace.

My life is certainly an example of the awesome, magnificent love of God. It is also an example of how low into degradation, sin and bondage one can descend when satanic power takes control of that life. My life also showcases the truth that there are indeed "NO HOPELESS CASES IN GOD'S EYES." The love of God had other plans for my life. Jer. 29:11 **"For I know the thoughts that I think toward you, saith the Lord, thoughts of peace, and not of evil, to give you an expected end."** The love of God had other plans for my life.

Psalm 107: 20 **"He sent His Word and healed them, and delivered them from their destructions."** The beginning of sorrows was the control the devil began to take in my childhood home. My story of deliverance is about demonic possession. There are many factors that I believe influence a child, or anyone for that matter, in falling into the devil's hands. I did not realize the power being exerted on me was demonic at that time. It was only after someone witnessed to me and explained to me that what I was going through was originating from the devil.

One very strong factor that I believe was an invitation for the devil to take control was the tumultuous home life I was subjected to. My father, an alcoholic who I watched beat my mother many times, upset me terribly. Evil spirits were certainly present and dominating the atmosphere in my home. Due to my father's bondage, he had a tremendous rage within him, which exploded anytime without notice. It would not be uncommon for him to explode at dinnertime and pull the tablecloth on the table violently out from underneath the food to be served and start throwing everything out the window. The turkey, the potatoes and all the trimmings went out the window. My Mom exclaimed, "Norman, what will the neighbors think?"

My sister and I looked at each other and asked, "What are we going to eat now?" We would sit there petrified of what might happen next. We were instructed to sit quietly and not say a word as my father looked at us filled with rage and anger. It would take days for things to get back to normal in the house. My mother tried to keep the peace and calm the atmosphere as she always was concerned about the effect this was having on my sister and me.

The Bible says in James 3:16, **"envy and strife in the household can open the door for every evil work."** My household was certainly a place of strife, hatred, anger, and oppression. I lived in fear on a daily basis. A spirit of fear took control over my life at a very early age. I became immersed in my studies and dedicated myself to perfection in all I would do, thinking that perfection would provide the solace my soul craved. I also determined that I would try to earn my father's love since I didn't get it naturally just being his daughter.

Emotional shock and sustained pressure creates access for the demonic also. I John 4:18 says, **"fear has torment."** I certainly lived in torment. It was manifested especially at night when I was sleeping and would be awakened with manifestations of evil at the foot of my bed. Many nights I would wake up seeing a figure with a black cloak standing at the foot of my bed. That was truly scary for an 11-year-old.

Another factor in the fertile environment for the devil to work in would be objects that represent demonic strongholds such as statues or images, which often constitute idols. It says in Deuteronomy 32: 16, **"They provoked God to jealousy with strange gods, with abominations provoked they him to anger."**

In the basement of our house there was a collection of swords that my father brought back from the war. No one liked the idea that they were down in the basement. They became something that people feared. I didn't know the reason why, but my father went down into the basement and spent long intervals there when he became irritated or depressed.

One very strong factor that affected the atmosphere in our home was the fact that someone had been murdered in the house before my parents bought it. Every night, when relaxing in the living room, my mother would tell us to listen to the strange visitor who would knock on the roof of the basement. It would be heard in the living room as 3 distinct knocks on the floor. That was something scary, at least for myself. My mom just passed it off as being our uninvited guest.

In other cases of demonic bondage generational idolatry and occult activity can set the stage for the devil's access. Unforgiveness can also contribute to demonic entrance. (See Matthew 18:34, 35.)

The words spoken in a home can also be a power for positive, spiritual blessings happening or destructive spirits being leashed into lives through negative declarations over lives. **"Death and life are in the power of the tongue."** Proverbs 18:21

CHAPTER 2

THE VOICE

The cords of hell encompassed me and the pangs of hell came upon me. I found trouble and sorrow.
Psalm 116: 3

When I was in eighth grade, I began to write notes to myself that said someone was going to kill me. Turmoil and depression set within me and I was disturbed by a voice that spoke to me. This was a very secret battle as I was considered a very bright student with a promising future. I was the type of student the teachers liked. I excelled in all my studies and there was within me a desire to somehow override the tormenting voice within me.

One day, as I was walking home from school, the battle within drew me completely into a tunnel of darkness and despair. John 10:10 says, **"The thief cometh not but for to steal and to kill, and to destroy, I am come that they may have life and that they might have it more abundantly."**

On this day, voices began to tell me to hurt myself physically. At first I thought it was crazy. I tried to push it out of my mind and thoughts. I rationalized with myself that this was an absurd, ridiculous idea, but the voice kept speaking and it became something that I could not just shrug off and forget about so I gave in. When I arrived home that day, I felt compelled by this voice to go to my mother's sewing box and I took a sewing needle and I swallowed it. That was the beginning of 7 long years in bondage to this satanic voice. As the Bible says, "to whom you yield yourself to that will become your master.." Every day was a battle that raged within me to see whether the voice within or my reasoning would win. No one knew the battle that raged within me. I was a bright student and my parents always received good reports about my behavior and my grades. During this period of time I found solace and protection hanging out in the Methodist church where I cleaned the communion cups. At this point in my life I felt totally insecure and afraid. I somehow felt protected when I was inside the church.

Now, after swallowing the sewing needle I was faced with the consequences of having to tell my mother and get medical help. What was I going to give as an excuse? Surely no one was going to believe me when I told them a voice told me to do it. After all, I was a very intelligent young girl who always received honors in school. I couldn't understand my behavior myself so how could I expect anyone else to understand? I began to fill up with more fear and anxiety.

I told my mother that I had swallowed a sewing needle

and I was taken to the emergency room where they x-rayed me and could see the needle. I was operated on and put in intensive care where they had an IV in my arm. The needle was located about 2 inches from my heart. When I recovered from the surgery again hearing that voice, I continued swallowing needles. The doctor was quite upset with me and warned my parents that he was quitting the case and they would have to obtain another doctor. My parents had to sign a release for another doctor to perform surgery and try to find another needle I had swallowed . They could not find the needle so it was left inside my body.

I was taken to the psychiatric ward of the hospital where they began to delve into the psychological working of my mind to try to understand why I was doing these things. I explained to the doctors that I felt like someone else was inside of me controlling my actions. I did not want to do the acts of self-inflicting harm, but I could not resist this power that was persuading me to do what I was doing. This voice brought anxiety to my heart, and then came a sense of helplessness that kept me bound for 7 long years, from 12 to 19 years old. The light grew dimmer and dimmer in this seemingly never-ending tunnel of defeat and despair.

The first treatment on the list from the psychiatrist was for me to be given electroshock therapy. They kept me at the mental ward and three times a week I would be led into a room down the hall walking barefoot. I felt as if I was being led to my electrocution. It was a very frightful experience as they shot me with some electricity in my brain and caused me to convulse. However, they had me half dazed but I could still see the lightning in the room. I had 18 of these treatments and they did not help the problem, they only caused me fear and anxiety. For many years after these treatments I was very much afraid of lightning. The electric shocks were supposed to block out bad memories, which they believed may have been influencing my behavior. The truth is you can't remove the devil with electric shocks. Thank God there is Someone who **"for that purpose was manifested to destroy the works of the devil."** I John 3:8

The only memories blocked out were some good memories. I began to have terrible nightmares that greatly tormented me at night. Visions of men in black cloaks appeared at the foot of my bed warning me that I would not live much longer.

I was taken to the psychiatrist regularly for therapy only to be asked the same questions repeatedly. "Why are you doing these things to yourself?" I told the doctor repeatedly that I did not want to do these things to myself but was being controlled by someone else inside of me. They didn't believe me. They tried to rationalize with me that if I continued this behavior I would more than likely kill myself. So psychiatric therapy for me was a long journey down a dead end street.

I remember in one therapy session the psychiatrist suggesting I become an alcoholic instead of hurting myself like I was doing. My response to him was, "If I had the ability to change my life I would pick something else." Obviously, they were trying to provide a natural solution to a spiritual problem. That's the best that man can do, offer a lesser bondage, but God brings freedom through Jesus Christ. John 8:36 **"Therefore if the Son shall make you free you shall be free indeed."**

It seemed that I would recover from one incident and then do something again and again. One day, I poured turpentine into my right eye. My eye was so injured I had to be taken to a special eye hospital located in Pennsylvania. I was fortunate not to lose my sight in that eye. After pouring turpentine into my eye

I kept the eye irritated and injured by rubbing it with objects and making it red all the time.

One night, when construction was taking place in the back of our house, I jumped from a platform and hurt my leg. Another time I threw myself down the stairs. One day, I was directed by this voice to take an electric knife and cut my hand. It required stitches and I was fortunate not to permanently injure my hand because of the ligaments and muscles that were injured. On another occasion, I drank a bottle of rubbing alcohol and it severely burned my stomach. Shortly after that I swallowed 30 aspirin. Thank God I recovered. God was merciful to me. However, I was truly in bondage to the voice that spoke to me and the power that wanted to destroy me.

I swallowed metal objects such as tops to soda cans, nuts, bolts, straight pins and safety pins. The doctor told my parents one day, "She has everything but the kitchen sink inside her."

One day, listening to this voice, I took eighteen pieces of razor blades, broke each one into two pieces, and I swallowed them. When the doctor x-rayed me, he said they were scattered through my entire digestive system and he would not consider operating because it would be massive. It was a miracle that all the razor blades passed through my system naturally. The doctors stated that I was very lucky for the razor blades to pass through my system without hurting me, but I know it was God's providential Hand reaching down. This was just one of many miracles to keep me alive to fulfill His Calling on my life.

One Sunday afternoon, my father told me to get in the car; he said we were going out. I thought maybe we were going for a ride in the country. When we pulled up to this very large, old building surrounded by other buildings and protected by tall, intimidating gates and fences, I knew we were not out for just a ride in the country. I was taken into a doctor's office and told I was going to be examined. I was told to remove all my clothes and then I was subjected to a very shameful, degrading unprofessional examination. The doctor spoke to me as if I had committed a crime and deserved to be punished. He repeatedly said, "Don't you know you are going to kill yourself by doing these self-inflicted acts? Is that what you want? Don't you see what you're doing to yourself?" I was then taken to housing for women. My first night was agonizing. There were about 8 other women in my ward and they were acting in a very psychotic manner. I would be woken at night to find some of them at the foot of my bed making weird sounds and grotesque faces. I was the youngest at only fifteen years old.

The next day, in this mental institution, a young man working on the grounds tried to sexually assault me. I reported it to my psychiatrist and he said to me, "Didn't you like it?" Not only was I enslaved in my own bondage, but I was trapped by the establishment of psychiatry that traced everything to sexual behavior.

Words of death and destruction spoken over me in this hospital and by other psychiatrists too planted more seeds of destruction. At the end of six weeks the doctors had a meeting with me and my parents and made the declaration that there was nothing they could do for me, there was no hope for me. They suggested that my parents put me away permanently because I would only wind up killing myself anyway.

They spoke man's wisdom, which had no hope, but God had plans **to prosper me and not harm me and give me hope and an expected future** as it says in Jer. 29:11. It was declared that there was no hope and they gave up, but God never gives up on us.

CHAPTER 3

FROM BAD TO WORSE

...the terrors of hell came upon me.

Ps 116: 3b

I drowned myself in my studies, making perfection my goal, which brought a sense of satisfaction and success, even though it was temporary, but I kept sinking deeper into the tunnel and kept inflicting pain and misery on myself. I also played the trumpet and found great peace and contentment in my music, even though that, too, was temporary. Through my academic accomplishments, I attained the privilege to be inducted into the National Honor Society in eighth grade and then again in high school into the High Honor Society. I took college prep classes as I felt that my only chance to make something of my life was to go to college and study and prepare for a profession. Little did I know that God had a plan for my life. Even the torturous life inflicted on me by the devil could not keep God from having His way with me.

As I look back on my life I can see the miraculous, merciful hand of God that sustained me. Even completing my studies was a miracle since I was physically unable to attend classes because of the frequent stays at the hospital dealing with the injuries I had inflicted on my body. But God made a way for me to have private teachers from the high school come to my house to give me the lessons. After God saved me I was so grateful I had graduated high school and pursued my studies despite my problems, especially since I would be seeking my theological degrees.

Even though I was immersed in my studies I was still filled with disillusionment, confusion, anxiety and depression. I was terrified mentally with the dreams, thoughts and compulsions the devil was filling me with.

For the next several years I began to inflict injury on my right leg, which eventually resulted in the destruction of the functioning of my right knee joint. Hearing this voice, I would take a sewing needle and hammer it into the right knee joint. I would then walk around with my knee hurting me and every day gradually getting worse. Finally, I would tell someone because I knew I needed medical help. I told my mother usually or a friend. Upon being examined at the hospital ER I was told I needed to be seen by an orthopedic surgeon to be operated on to remove the needle. This was the beginning of a long season of damaging the knee joint of my right leg, which gradually affected the whole leg.

When the orthopedic doctor looked at the x-ray, he showed us how the needle was in the place where it would cause the most damage. After several years of doing the same thing the doctor said the needles could not have been more precisely placed, almost as if a surgeon put them there, in the place that would cause the most damage. Surely the enemy knew the precise place of maximum destruction to my leg. Even though the devil did these acts with diabolical precision, God's plan and purposes are even more precise as God did not let the devil destroy me.

God surely had a plan for my life. He had already marked me for His Divine purposes. He was truly merciful to me. Many people refer to my testimony as "the testimony of needles," but I am quick to tell them it is truly a "testimony of the mercy of God."

I seemed to have slipped into a pattern at this time. I would put a needle in my knee and a surgeon would remove it and after the operation put my leg in a cast. This went on for about 12-15 operations and a total of 17 surgical procedures on my leg and knee. I had 24 surgeries and procedures total from the swallowing events and leg injuries I caused. I went through severe infections and high fevers and almost lost my life several times. I finally developed a bone disease called osteomyelitis. Because of the disease I would require surgeries and draining of the knee joint because of the severity of the infections. It became harder and harder to deal with the pain.

One time, after being operated on and my leg placed in a cast as usual, listening to this voice, I opened the window of the cast and took some of the dirty material from my mattress and poked it into the incision in my leg. My leg became severely inflamed and even more infected. I remember the doctor being very unhappy with me. On other occasions, I would open the incision and I would put dirt or other foreign material in it, making the infection worse. Many times, surgeries would be required to drain my leg of all the debris and drains had to be placed into my leg. During this period I would spend weeks in the hospital with IV antibiotics. The doctors kept telling my parents,

"Holly is going to lose her leg if she keeps this up." But God was merciful to me.

Many times, doctors believed amputation was imminent but God preserved my leg. He was truly merciful to me. There were doctors who refused to operate on me or take care of me, but there was one doctor, at Monmouth Medical Center, who pledged his loyalty to care for me until the day I didn't do those things anymore. His attitude gave me hope that there was a doctor who would stick with me. He believed there would be an end.

My body was slowly wearing down. My immune system could barely keep up with the constant mutilation and poisoning that was shocking my system. Doctors even felt my system was becoming immune to antibiotics. As if my personal agony emotionally and physically wasn't severe enough, doctors and nurses would giggle outside my door, saying, "Do you want to see the crazy girl who swallows needles?" I was so ashamed. I became the laughing stock of the hospital. I felt like I was on display in the devil's circus menagerie. However, it wouldn't be too long before I would be learning about full acceptance and being translated from the kingdom of darkness into the kingdom of His dear Son.

We have a high priest who was touched with the feelings of our infirmities yet without sin. Jesus experienced rejection at Calvary being rejected of men and acquainted with grief. Men mocked Him and taunted Him on the cross. He can comfort you in all your trials. The atonement at Calvary is complete to restore you in every aspect of your life. I'm living proof of the power of the resurrected Savior.

After a long stay with multiple infections and a month of IV antibiotics, I was sent home once again with a large cast and a window in it so the doctor could treat the wound at the incision site. I was walking on crutches. I remember being extremely depressed and feeling there was absolutely no hope for me. The psychologist was still trying to convince me to stop hurting myself. I kept telling him I didn't want to do these things but I felt as if I was being controlled by a power on the inside of me. One of his recommendations was to broaden my social life and get a boyfriend. I remember telling him, "No, not now, dealing with the complexities of the problem I have is quite enough."

One day, I felt compelled to go down into the basement and I was directed by the voice to take nails and hammer them into the incision in my already badly wounded leg. I followed the order and the next thing I knew I was waking up from having fainted. I walked around for several days because I felt at this point I just couldn't stand the ridicule and the questions. Probably due to the pain, I fainted again and my mom knew something was up and I was taken back to the hospital. The prognosis was I would most probably lose my leg.

Doctors rushed me back into the operating room for a long operation removing pieces of nail and finally a section of bone that the nails were hammered into. I woke up from the operation in great fear but, to my surprise, my leg was still there. Again, God was merciful to me.

Through the years my leg continued to deteriorate and the knee joint weakened until it became useless and there was no other choice but to remove the knee joint and require me to wear a built-up shoe because the leg would be 2 inches shorter. The doctors removed my knee joint and fused the two leg bones together. After this surgery, I had to learn to walk all over again. Little did I know that what I was doing in the natural I would soon do in the Spirit, as God showed me a new way to walk.

I still have 5 needles in my body that could not be removed: One needle in each of the following areas of my body:

1. Chest cavity
2. Gall Bladder
3. Base of spine
4. Left leg
5. Right leg

People tell me needles can travel through the body. My response is, "Needles may travel but these are not the traveling kind; they have no passport or visa." In other words, God has His Almighty, All Powerful Hand upon my life. They have been in the same place and have not caused me any problems.

The only problem occurs when I get x-rays in the hospital and they all go crazy when they see the needles. They change their course of action and forget about what I went in there for. Because of that, I resist going to the doctors or the hospital. Also, because of the ridiculing I received for years from the medical profession, it made it hard for me to go to them. God has amazingly taken care of me.

However, there was an anesthetist who went on one of our mission trips and God put it on his heart to talk to me about my reluctance to trust the medical profession. I'm grateful to Tony Smith for ministering to me in this way at that very needful time in my life. He even went with me to see a doctor to break the ice. I do go to the doctor if I really need to now. However, I am never in any rush to get there.

Ephesians 2:10 **"For we are His workmanship, created in Christ Jesus unto good works, which God hath before ordained that we should walk in them."**

Although it is not common for people to hear the devil's voices to destroy them to this extent, the voices of sin, despair and the worldly system still draw countless multitudes whom the god of this world has blinded. Jesus is the same yesterday, today and forever. He saves, heals and can deliver you from any bondage no matter how great! The testimony of Jesu is the Spirit of Prophecy. I believe this testimony to Jesus' glorious power and mercy can give you the faith to believe for God's miraculous power in your life. No obstacle of sin, disease, poverty, hopelessness or bondage is too great for the Lord to break through and transform you. Jesus came to give us life, and life more abundantly.

CHAPTER 4

MY 'CRAZY NEIGHBOR'

**Then called I upon the name of the Lord;
oh Lord, I beseech thee, deliver my soul. Gracious is the Lord and righteous, yea our God is
merciful.
The Lord preserveth the simple. I was brought
low and He helped me.**

Ps. 116:4-6

Our kitchen in our house faced our neighbor's kitchen. I remember her singing and praying and praising God.

When I am preaching, I like to remind people not to be ashamed to lift their voices wherever they are and give praise and glory to God. There is power in praise! Many times, when I'm out in the stores, I'll

35

be worshipping or singing or speaking in tongues and if there is another Christian nearby they will say, "Amen," and join in with me. On many occasions, it also opens the door to minister to someone. Praise prepares the atmosphere for a powerful witness. Our public worship is a testimony to the Lord and our love for Him. It seemed like my neighbor was always praying and praising God. I said to my mom, "Listen to the crazy neighbor."

The audacity of my calling this dear intercessor crazy. Surely MY behavior could have been characterized as crazy. So often the Truth of God is deemed 'crazy' by the world.

...Titus 1:15 **"Unto the pure all things are pure. But unto them that are defiled and unbelieving is nothing pure, but even their mind and conscience is defiled."**

God had placed that woman of God, you might say, "in my back yard," to complete a divine assignment to pray and intercede for my deliverance. God had already spoken to her and it bore witness to Jeremiah 1:5: **"Before I formed you in the womb I knew you. And before you were born I consecrated you. I have appointed you a prophet to the nations."**

Find your place in God's kingdom. God has a place for you.

He is counting on you occupying the post He has called you to. There may be several reasons why you are not in your place. I believe one of those reasons is people do not believe that God could use them. One of the very profound Biblical truths is that God uses imperfect vessels. Let me remind you of a few: David was a humble shepherd but he committed adultery and murder. God said he had a heart after the heart of God. Why? He failed so many times. He was so imperfect. But he was also a man who knew the power of repentance and developed an intimacy with God through worship. Esther, another imperfect vessel, married to a Gentile, was used by God to save her people from a massacre. Mathew was a tax collector and a very unpopular individual and a symbol of the oppression of Israel. God transformed him and used him as an Apostle and the writer of the first New Testament book.

If these individuals had to measure up to the corporate bureaucratic scrutiny to be selected for a job in one of our major corporations today, they would not have been selected. Their resumes would not have borne the marks of "most likely to succeed".

God works by different standards. He chooses the most unlikely, ill-prepared candidates with no prior experience or excellence, even taking them out of the pigpen of sin and transforming them, and then uses them as He converts their problems, bondages and addictions and hopelessness into testimonies to the glory and power of God.

I'm one of those privileged ones, honored that God should overturn the prognosis of the doctors and send someone to live right next to me for seven years to pray for my deliverance because He had a destiny for me to fulfill. I may have a Doctorate in Theology and a few other degrees, but I'm honored and highly favored of the Lord to be called a Servant of God and, even though I earned my degrees fulfilling requirements for each one, I could never earn the right or privilege to be called a Servant of God.

This neighbor certainly knew her place and she lived to see the fruit produced from faithful prayer. Years passed, more than seven. Seven long years in a tunnel of darkness, fear, rejection, bondage and helplessness with hopelessness that seemed like all eternity having to go through it day by day. She kept praying and believing for a miracle in my life, a miracle of deliverance and salvation.

How often do God's people give up prior to the victory? Perseverance in prayer is necessary. Don't stop praying and believing for that loved one you think is hopeless. Many times, God will take us to the midnight hour before our breakthrough because He is not only interested in the person you are praying for but His purpose is to mature and perfect you in the Spirit. We must die to our wills and live for His purposes pressing on to the mark of the high call in Jesus Christ.

The Lord has His intercessors dispersed throughout the earth praying for the victory over people and nations. We must press through and endure to see His kingdom come on Earth as it is in heaven. We need to be like a trumpet praying in the Spirit for the Lord's breakthrough. However, to be a true intercessor, and to be in the Spirit, the Lord must often consign us to our own Patmos, which means the killing of self. We must die daily bearing our cross and living to do His will. Luke 9:23 "If anyone wishes to come after me, let him deny himself, take up his cross and follow me."

One day, my neighbor, Mrs. Erhart, came to my house knocking on my door. I quickly notified my mom that the 'crazy' neighbor was coming. She had never come to our house before. God's timing is perfect; He knows when people are ready. The ground of the human heart must be ready to bring forth fruit. Wow, God's love, it's so rich and reaches to the lowliest and knows no boundaries: I was making fun of His servant and He still reached out to me. Oh, how He loves you and me! She invited me to a young people's meeting in someone's house. I accepted the invitation because I was bored of being shut up in the house walking on crutches and having nowhere to go. However, God had another purpose that would be life-changing. The life and invitation of this neighbor mightily transformed my thinking and even as a Christian I realize the importance of being led by the Holy Spirit and obeying opportunities for divine appointments, realizing I may be the key to a breakthrough in someone's life.

In my darkness, I didn't realize God had sent this neighbor to pray for me. When I received my deliverance and gave my life to the Lord, God called me to Bible School. I went next door to say goodbye to my neighbor. I found her amid boxes and luggage and I told her I came to say goodbye because I was leaving for Bible School and she began to cry and worship God. Noticing all the boxes and luggage, I asked her if she too was going somewhere. She said to me, "My work is done here. God sent me here to pray for you." We rejoiced together now that my eyes were opened and I could appreciate her sacrifice and commitment to pray for me. She had successfully completed her assignment.

I am so thankful that my neighbor obeyed the Holy Spirit and accepted the challenge to intercede on my behalf. My bondage required some serious intercession and a commitment to fight the spiritual battles that would be the result of her engagement in the war going on in my life. She understood the depth of spiritual warfare taking place in my house when she heard the rages of my father and witnessed the turkey being thrown out the window.

The ministry of intercession is often obscured from the world's attention, not receiving the praise of man, but God knows these important saints who are crucial to the Lord's purposes. Surely many of these intercessors who have shed tears and borne the burdens in the secret place for the salvation of future evangelists and pastors and others in ministry will receive that tap on the shoulder and hear, "Well done, thou good and faithful servant." Even though they are overlooked on Earth and sometimes misunderstood and criticized, many will be brought to the forefront in heaven. Matthew 20:16 **"So the last shall be first, and the first last; for many are called, but few chosen."** Man will often exalt what God thinks is unimportant. It is important for us to place value on what God finds important and to prioritize according to God's priorities.

CHAPTER 5

A RAY OF HOPE

…the Lord hath dealt bountifully with thee.
Ps 116:7

A ray of hope burst forth at this young people's meeting. The day came to go with my neighbor to this meeting in someone's home. She was dropping me off at the house since it was a young people's meeting. I felt a little uneasy but I kept reminding myself that what I felt was nothing compared to the despair and disillusionment I felt daily. Little did I know I was being taken to a divine appointment that would change me and my world forever. This appointment was also an introduction to me about God's divine appointments, which I would come to understand better as time went on and the

Holy Spirit began to work intensely in my heart and life.

Early on I knew that my calendar of human appointments had to be subject to change for the divine alternative. Now I look for and welcome divine appointments. That does not mean that the schedule on my calendar was not pleasing to God, it just means God is interrupting my schedule. He's up to something. That's when things get exciting. From that point on I began to look forward to God's divine interruptions and appointments in my life. When God interrupts, the ordinary becomes supernatural. Truly it became obvious that the ray of hope at the meeting would be my journey from the natural to the supernatural. This meeting was the first stage that brought to me a ray of hope.

I had no idea what to expect at this meeting. I knew it would be "religious" in nature but I was ignorant of anything else to expect. All my prior experience with "religion" had been in the Methodist and Episcopal churches. However, from the moment I walked into the living room it was obvious that my "divine appointment" was in the form of a person and not a program or anything I had known in the "religious" world.

At this meeting, I met my ray of hope. She was a Bible teacher who became my mentor and spiritual mother, Nancy Stein. Just by watching her read from a book about Nicky Cruz I could see in her eyes and the expression on her face that her countenance was different. It was full of hope and joy. She radiated, it seemed, with the glow of an electric light bulb. I would soon learn that this was the Presence of God. Something drew me to focus not so much on the surroundings or the content of the book but on her countenance, which seemed to draw its strength from another realm. I was drawn to Nancy and not the book she was reading; everything and everyone seemed unimportant compared to what was flowing from this woman. She radiated with joy and peace, which gave me a reason to keep watching her.

I sat there not paying any attention to the testimony she was reading but with my eyes fixed on her, wondering how it was possible to have such peace and joy when my life was so miserable. I was embarrassed to talk to her among the group of young people yet inside I yearned to pour my heart out to her. I left the meeting that night wishing I could sit down and talk with her, but little did I realize my divine appointment was just a day away. The Holy Spirit was talking to Nancy as He was preparing my heart also. She invited me to come to her house and talk with her the following day. Again, not that I needed another confirmation about the special touch of God on her life; however, I was firmly convinced she was communicating to an all-powerful source who I knew nothing about. However, I was about to become a disciple and student of this 'strange' woman that I admired. God was drawing me through Nancy with "His strong cords of love."

2 Corinthians 3:3 **"Forasmuch as ye are manifestly declared to be the epistle of Christ ministered by us, written not with ink, but with the Spirit of the living God, not in tables of stone, but in fleshly tablets of the heart."**

Psalm 18:16 **"He sent from above, He took me, He drew me out of many waters."**

The next chapter will give you an idea of the gifted mentor God sent to me in the person of Nancy Stein as you come along with me on the part of the journey that led to the "revolution and deliverance" in my devil-torn and weary life. She certainly was a ray of hope shining forth to let me know there are never too many broken pieces for God to fix. So amazing is God's love and power that when He puts all the broken pieces back together and adds new pieces, He makes something beautiful. He truly takes our brokenness and exchanges it for beauty.

Nancy would be the vessel God would use, and she became, for a period of time, the most important person in my life. She would bring the message of hope to my world of despair and broken pieces. She would bring clarity, purpose and destiny to my life, which was deep in the pit and snare of the evil one. Without speaking a word, her countenance, expressions and mannerisms brought a ray of hope to my life. For the first time, I dared to believe that there could be an escape route from my long, dark, unending tunnel of despair. I started thinking that maybe my appointment with Nancy could be the beginning of a new day.

So many Christians complain that they have no techniques for soul winning, but don't be discouraged; the light and the love and joy of Christ emanating through our eyes and countenance can often do far more than the most perfect theological lecture on salvation. The following Scriptures demonstrate that as believers we carry the greatest treasure of all, the Spirit of Christ in our earthly vessels, "Christ in us the Hope of Glory." Let HIM shine through you! 2 Corinthians 4:6 **"For God, who commands the light to shine out of darkness, hath shined in our hearts to give the light of the knowledge of the glory of God in the face of Jesus Christ."**

2 Corinthians 4:7 **"But we have this treasure in earthen vessels, that the excellency of the power may be of God, and not of us."**

Believers need divine appointments so they can show-case the glory of God. I'm sure Nancy was praying for me that a door would open giving her the opportunity to minister to me. Being the Spirit-filled and powerful believer she was I know she looked for those God-given opportunities to show off the glory of God. Romans 8:14 tells us, **"For as many as are led by the**

Spirit of God, they are the sons of God."

Living in the Spirit enables the believer to be led to key places and meet people with discernment in their hearts. Perhaps words of knowledge and wisdom will flow resulting from obedience to the appointment. The love of Christ will also flow, when we cease to strive and enter into His rest, where God works through a yielded vessel.

Truly God was working through his yielded servant and He continued to work as we began the miraculous journey into the "Dawning of a New Day".

I ended that first encounter with his servant that night with a heart full of hope and a glimmer of the Light of the World shining into my dark tunnel of despair. JUST MAYBE THERE WAS HOPE FOR ME.

CHAPTER 6

THE DAWNING OF A NEW DAY AND MY MENTOR

"Gracious is the Lord, and righteous, yes our God is compassionate."

Ps. 116:5

T he day of my divine appointment had arrived. I was very excited all through the night and it was the first thing that came to my mind in the morning. This was the day I would speak to this woman who had made such an impression on my life. She came in her car to pick me up, and off we went to her friend's house where we had met with the youth the night before. I couldn't stop watching her, she had such a beautiful expression on her face and, again, just like the night before, she was radiating like a light bulb. She had big, brown eyes and they were full of love and compassion. For the first time I felt free to tell a total stranger about all of my bondage and the voice that drove me. Much to my surprise, she didn't mock me as others had. This pleased me and gave me even more confidence to keep talking to her. Even after the litany of severe torment, bondage, mutilation and resultant surgeries and treatments she insisted confidently and authoritatively that there was hope not only for survival but for an abundant life.

She said to me, "Holly, that voice that is speaking to you is the voice of the devil and he is trying to destroy your life. However, there's SOMEONE ELSE and His Name is JESUS CHRIST, He is the Son of God, the Savior of the World, the Giver of Life, and He has more power than all the power of the devil." Acts 10:38 **"God anointed Jesus of Nazareth with the Holy Spirit and with power, and He went about**

doing good and healing all that were sick and op-pressed of the devil; for God was with Him."

She continued. "If you repent of your sins and sur-render your life to Him, He will save you, transform you, liberate you and give you a new life." Never be-fore had anyone spoken such words of hope to me.

Not only did she speak such words of hope and en-couragement but she spoke them with such love and concern. She showed deep sympathy to me. That was truly a different attitude than I was used to previously. I told Nancy that all the doctors and psychiatrists had told me I was a "lost cause."

I questioned her statement that there could be hope for me to change.

There was no hope and no way out I thought. After years and years of listening to lies from 'trained pro-fessionals' that's what I believed.

I really believed that I was a lost cause. I did not believe that there was an answer to my problem, until then. That day, a ray of hope shone on my life even if it seemed to be in the distance. Everything Nancy was saying was like water on the dry ground, a light at the end of a long dark tunnel.

For so many years my heart had yearned to hear this kind of news. I began to get excited just hearing the possibilities Nancy spoke about. I could see the reality of what she spoke evidenced in her life.

The reality of her faith was all over her; in her eyes, voice, in her expression and tone of her voice.

All the while she spoke to me I was thinking, *How wonderful if this is true and there is hope for me. I could be like her and have the peace and joy that flowed out from her life.* I was imagining even having the smile that she wore.

I asked Nancy, "Is this what you have?"

She said "Yes. If you see any good in me, it's Jesus Christ. He is my joy, my peace and my reason for living."

She asked me if she could pray with me and if I would make that surrender of my life to the Lord. I said to her, "Yes, but one question I have. Will I get your smile too?"

She said, "Yes you will have a smile too because Jesus will fill you with His joy."

I must add here; I don't understand Christians who never seem to have joy. When I preach, I tell them, "Your smile is the way you showcase God's salvation and His joy unspeakable and full of glory." I've had this smile since 1969 and it just gets bigger and bigger and people admire my smile and it opens the door to witness to them. I always think of Nancy and her smile and how it made such an enduring impression on my life.

The truth to be told is that smiling makes me feel better too. I know now, "The joy of the Lord is my strength."

Nancy led me through Scripture explaining the path to salvation. The following are some of those important salvation Scriptures:

Mark 1:5 **"The time is fulfilled and the kingdom of God is at hand: repent ye, and believe the gospel."**

Romans 3:23 **"For all have sinned and come short of the glory of God."**

Romans 6:23 **"The wages of sin is death; but the gift of God is eternal life through the Lord Jesus Christ."**

Nancy explained how we are all sinners in need of the Savior. Adam and Eve were placed in the garden of Eden and everything for them was perfect. God told them not to eat of the Tree of Knowledge but

the devil came and tempted Eve and they yielded to
the devil and disobeyed God. Because of that, sin
entered the human race and a sentence of death, but
God provided a Savior, His Son, Jesus Christ, to lay
down His life for you and me to be redeemed from
the curse the law brought.

John 3:16 **"For God so loved the world that He
gave His only begotten son that whoever believes
in Him should not perish but have everlasting
life."**

As Nancy began to pray for me I could feel the supernatural power of God reaching down into my life. It
felt like an earthquake was taking place in my body. It
seemed like God was moving things around. I began
to ask for forgiveness and repent of my sins. I prayed
the sinner's prayer. I immediately could feel the peace
of God.

Then Nancy quoted Romans 10:9-10 **"If thou shalt
confess with thy mouth the Lord Jesus and shall**

believe in thine heart that God hath raised him from the dead, thou shalt be saved. For with the heart man believeth unto righteousness, and with the mouth confession is made unto salvation."

Nancy prayed a prayer of deliverance from demonic bondage. Having experienced the power of the devil, I knew this was different from anything I had ever experienced in my heart or life. It became evident that this was just the beginning of a journey to complete deliverance and under Nancy's ministry I would in the future experience many sessions of her praying over me and releasing the power of God to bring me to the next stage. I embraced everything she taught me in the following two years. There were many strongholds in my life and each had to be dealt with, but the relationship I had with Jesus from day one was so wonderful I now understood what I was facing and what was left to be overcome in my life.

Madam Jeanne Guyon said, "As you come to Him, come as a weak child, one who is all soiled and badly bruised – a child that has been hurt from falling again. Come to the Lord as one who has no strength of his own, come to him as one who has not power to cleanse himself. Humbly lay your pitiful condition before your Father."

Even though it was a journey, it was now a journey being walked out by someone who had left the satanic kingdom and was fast gaining headway into being completely whole. I was no longer in a tunnel but was on a journey to total freedom and a new life. It was now an adventure because I rejoiced because of the life I left behind and I was hopeful and optimistic looking ahead at what God had planned for me, not only in my deliverance but in fulfilling His purposes for me on this earth for the future. Nancy would always remind me of Jeremiah 1:5. **"Before I formed you in the womb I knew you, and before you were born I consecrated you; I have appointed you as a prophet to the nations."**

Little did I know or could even fathom I would be traveling to 15 countries to preach and prophesy the Word of the Living God. Nancy shared with me at several points in time along the journey that God had revealed to her that He had a call upon my life and that she was to work with me and minister to me.

Nancy told me I now needed the Word of God for complete and long-term deliverance from the devil's bondage. She said over and over again, "Holly, There's power in the Word of God." Romans 10:17 **"So then faith cometh by hearing, and hearing by the Word of God."**

She said I needed to go to church. She came in her car and took me to every service. That was an extra half hour each way for her. I had decided at that point that I wanted in my life what Nancy had. I wanted the depth of a relationship with the Lord like she had. I wanted the power and authority and peace and joy that she had. I wanted it all at once but I soon learned that it was a process requiring my surrender, commitment and discipline in the things of God.

The Word of God is the secret to victory. Nancy was always quoting the Bible. Whenever I would ask her a question, she would always say, "Let's see what the Word of God says." She said, "The permanence of your deliverance is in the power of the Word of God." I needed to get filled up with God's Word now, she said.

She referred to the story in Matthew 12:43,44. **"When the unclean spirit is gone out of a man, he walketh through dry places, seeking rest and findeth none. Then he saith, I will return unto my house from whence I came out, and when he is come, he findeth it empty, swept and garnished."**

The devil, she assured me, would try to come back. You see the evil spirits go through dry places, the wet places overflowing with the Water of the Word and the Spirit are not places for his dwelling. Soon the journey to deliverance and stability in my new Christian life began. Nancy assured me that II Corinthians 5:17 would be a reality.

"If any man be in Christ, he is a new creature and old things are passed away; behold, all things are become new."

She kept saying over and over, "The Word of God is your deliverance. The Word of God is your deliverance."

She then mentored me week by week besides taking me to church with her. I wanted what she had so badly. I admired her knowledge of the Scriptures. She was self-taught and, of course, taught by the Holy Spirit. She was my inspiration to the life I was pursuing, which I'd never thought was possible because all that ever had been spoken over me was gloom and doom.

When we were at the church services, I sat next to her and I watched her intently and I imitated her. My logic was I would try to imitate her to get what she had. Truly childlike ways they were. Somehow I believe God translated my actions into hunger for Him and later He would teach me that it's not just about imitating someone but doing the things such as the devotional disciplines that produced this spirituality in her life. But in the meantime, in a childlike fashion but with a sincere heart, I stood up when she stood up and I raised up my hands in worship when she did. I listened to her pray and tried to copy her. When she went to the altar for prayer after the service when everyone gathered around to wait on God, I followed her to the altar. About a year later, at the same altar, God baptized me in the Holy Spirit.

Nancy took her call to mentor and disciple me seriously. We need more mentors in the church. Mentors are like coaches. They lead the way and coach us along to follow, addressing the needs that occur on the journey, uplifting and encouraging us on the way, picking us up when we fall and encouraging us when we get discouraged over our progress. A mentor must be a very positive person.

The Scriptures instruct us about mentoring in the Book of Titus.

2:3-5 **"Older women likewise are to exhibit behavior fitting for those who are holy, not slandering, not slaves to excessive drinking, but teaching what is good. In this way they will train the younger women to love their husbands, to love their children, to be self-controlled, pure, fulfilling their duties at home, kind, being subject to their own husbands, so that the message of God may not be discredited."**

Mentoring involves a friendship relationship based on faithfulness, commitment and accountability on the part of the mentee and the mentor must be a person of spiritual maturity, faith and Godly conduct. A mentor should know the basic doctrines of the Bible. Nancy taught me how to research topics together with her. She would always say the best answers for life's questions and problems are found in the Bible. She would give me lunch and she would teach me line upon line how to research together to find the answers from God's Word.

2 Timothy 2:15 **"Study to shew thyself approved unto God, a workman that needeth not to be ashamed, rightly dividing the word of truth."**

The Apostle Paul said that his followers should look to him as an example in the same way that he looked to Christ. (1 Corinthians 11:1)

Nancy was my "Paul" and I looked to her as my example. She was someone who not only "gave a teaching", but her life was a living example of the teaching. That's where the power of God is. The words written on paper come alive when someone lives by those words and applies them to their life on a daily basis.

"Whatever you have learned or received or heard from me, or seen in me—put it into practice" Philippians 4:9. In essence, he is saying, "Let me mentor you. Let me be your role model." He reminds the new Christians at Thessalonica to "follow our example" 2 Thessalonians 3:7. Example. Teach. Model. These are all phases of mentoring that are very important in developing fully devoted followers of Jesus and in transmitting the faith from one generation to the next. It goes without saying that if mentors expect others to follow their example, they must be untangled with the world and fully committed to following Christ.

Not only Jesus and the Apostles but elders in the local church also do their work by mentoring. Peter commands, **"Be examples to the flock"** 1 Peter 5:3, and Paul explains to the elders at Ephesus, **"You know how I lived the whole time I was with you"** Acts 20:17. In other words, Paul is telling the elders,

"I showed you, now you show them." In all truth, if a Christian leader is not mentoring someone, to that degree he or she is not living up to his or her calling.

I believe part of sustaining a move of God in the local church is the church body and leadership fostering the placement of mentors within the different departments of the church, having been approved by leadership to do this type of "spiritual coaching" to believers. The mentors should meet with leadership occasionally and make sure they are on the same page as far as vision and spiritual practices, making sure they are in alignment with church doctrine.

The church should also provide training for mentors. Being a mentor is not a position of authority, it is a position of coaching. Mentoring is needed on different levels, such as beginners and those called to ministry and those who are ministering. As I began my journey with Nancy, when I received ministerial licensing and ordination, my need for mentoring on a different level changed.

Nancy was my coach and she was totally committed to her Lord and Savior. No matter how many years I served the Lord, she was always there to encourage me and many times teach me because she had a very advanced knowledge of the Word of God.

It would be easy to understand how I became very dependent on Nancy. She was so strong in every sense of the word. I was just a babe in the Lord and Nancy was like a giant to me.

I was dealing with the strongholds of fear and condemnation and she always made me soar in the heavenlies. I was sorry for the years of self-inflicted agony I brought on myself, even though it was the devil. Nancy showed me in the Scriptures how I could be free from the tormenting spirit of fear and condemnation. She told me to declare the victory by telling the devil what the Word of God says: Romans 8:1

"There is therefore no condemnation for those who are in Christ Jesus."

She would rebuke the devil and the spirit of condemnation would leave. I was definitely leaning on her strength and pulling from her victory. Fear would come over me that I may not succeed in having the kind of victory she had. I couldn't imagine going back to being how I was before.

2 Timothy 1:7 **"For God has not given us a spirit of fear, but of power and of love and of a sound mind."** She would tell me, "You just tell the devil you don't accept that spirit of fear in Jesus' name. There is power in the Word of God. Stand by faith on God's Word and the Holy Spirit will manifest to bring you victory." And over and over again she emphasized to me, "There's power in the Word of God." Not only did Nancy teach and disciple me, but she encouraged me. One of the ways she encouraged me was by reading the hymns and telling me the stories of their

authors and how they came to write the hymns. These were very powerful and anointed times at her kitchen table. One day, I arrived very upset and discouraged and she went and got the hymnbook she had on her shelf. She began to relate to me how when she was feeling discouraged, she would read many times the hymns and she brought my attention to the hymn

"It Is Well With My Soul". "When peace like a river, attendeth my way, when sorrows like sea billows roll, Whatever my lot, Thou hast taught me to say, 'It is well, it is well, with my soul.

It is well, it is well, It is well, with my soul.'"

Horatio Spafford wrote as a prelude to his famous hymn, "Psalm 34:19" **"Many are the afflictions of the righteous but the Lord delivers him out of them all."**

Horatio had planned a trip to attend the meetings of D.L. Moody and Ira Sankey, with whom he was very good friends. His wife and daughters were going with him. However, an urgent matter prevented him from leaving with his family so he sent them ahead, settling them in a cabin aboard the French liner Ville du Havre. The ship was hit by another ocean liner and, in two hours, despite the screams and the prayers of the people they were buried in the depths of an icy ocean in a nightmare of immeasurable terror. From the ravages of brokenheartedness and despair came this hymn, which has been sung in churches all over the world by people coming to grips with some agonizing event of their own.

I felt secure and protected from the devil when I was with Nancy and receiving from her anointed teachings. She was quick to point out to me that, no matter how deep the sorrow or agonizing the pain, when you are a child of God, "it is well with my soul. Whatever my lot, thou hast taught me to say it is well it is well with my soul."

CHAPTER 7

SHOWDOWN WITH THE DEVIL

**"For thou hast delivered my soul from death,
Mine eyes from tears and my feet from falling."**
Psalm 116:8

God did a major overhaul in my heart when I surrendered my life to Jesus and accepted Him as my Lord and Savior. My deliverance was an ongoing process; it was not instantaneous. There were still many mountains to climb and rivers to cross. However, I was no longer in the boat by myself. I now had a destination and a determination to be complete as a child of God. However, I battled against condemnation and fear. I was very sorry for the mutilation of my body. I condemned myself for my behavior. **"But God hath not given me a spirit** of fear, but of power and of a sound mind." 2 Timothy 1:7 Nancy would assure me of God's forgiveness and tell me, "If God has forgiven you, who are you to condemn yourself?" **"If we confess our sins, He is faithful and just to forgive us our sins, and to cleanse us from all unrighteousness."** I John 1:9

I had to learn to take this Scripture and believe it just as if it had my name on it. II Corinthians 5:17

"If any man be in Christ, he is a new creature. Old things are passed away. Behold all things are become new."

Some days this Scripture just seemed like a wonderful dream and other days it seemed like a reality. I had to learn not to live by my feelings but by the truth of the Word of God.

God has given me a mind that has been delivered, rescued, and revived. When I yielded to condemnation, fear took over because it seemed like a long road to reach the kind of faith and power that Nancy had. One night, as I prepared for bed for the night, the devil said to me, "You're not really saved. You are bad. God would never forgive you." It was obvious that demonic forces were contending to keep a foothold in my mind and life. My mind went back to one night when I was in the hospital and still under psychiatric care even though I had begun my new life in Christ. The officials were contending my case with the doctors concerning assigning me to a mental institution for good. Nancy called a couple of intercessors and they broke the bands of the enemy and his assignment to destroy my future, and even my life, using the Scripture as their weapon. It worked. They were not able to get a ruling by the court to put me away.

At first I felt very much afraid when the devil began speaking to me. My immediate instinct led me to run to my parents' bedroom where there was a telephone and call Nancy. I called, but the line was busy. As I walked back to my bedroom the Holy Spirit said to me, "USE MY WORD, THERE'S POWER IN MY WORD."

I thought to myself without saying it, *Well, now I'm going to see if this teaching of Nancy's really works.* I thought about the many lessons at her kitchen table and the Scriptures began to roll through my head. It was different now though. I was used to Nancy, my spiritual mother and my mentor, rebuking the devil and declaring the Word of God. Would the devil respond to me as he did to the woman of God? I was just a babe in the Lord. Well, I found out that night it had nothing to do with Nancy or me but with the power of the spoken Word of God.

Power and authority come from the Word, the name of Jesus and the blood of Jesus. I returned to my bedroom and I picked up my Bible and began to declare to the devil, "Devil, the Bible ***says,*** **'You are a liar**

and the father of lies.' John 8:44 I am a child of God.

"John 1:12 **'But as many as received him, to them gave He the power to become the sons of God, even to them that believe on his name.'** I have confessed with my mouth and believed in my heart that Jesus is the Son of God, so devil I am a child of God.

"Devil, I belong to God now.

"I am washed in the Blood of Jesus.

"Ephesians 1:7 **'In whom we have redemption through his blood, the forgiveness of sins, according to the riches of his grace.'**

"Devil, my sins are gone. What can wash away my sin? Nothing but the blood of Jesus."

I became very aware of the presence of the Holy Spirit and I knew it was God bearing witness to His Word and He was coming against the dark thoughts and railing against the accusations the devil was throwing at me.

I John 1:9 **"If we confess our sins He is faithful and just to forgive us our sins and cleanse us of all unrighteousness."**

John 8:32 **"And ye shall know the truth, and the truth shall make you free."**

1John 3:8 **"For this purpose was the Son of God manifested to destroy the works of the devil."**

James 4:7 **"Submit yourselves therefore to God. Resist the devil and he will flee."**

As I continued to resist the devil by declaring the Word of God, the teaching of my mentor became a reality. I declared, "Devil, in the name of Jesus, through the power of the Word of God and the anointing of the Holy Spirit I put you under my feet. You no longer have control over my life.

"For me to live is Christ.

"I John 4:4 **'Greater is He that is in ME than he that is in the world.'**

"I am a child of God; I am an overcomer not by my own strength but by the great and glorious God who is within me! Romans 8:31-39, devil, hear the Word of God:

'What shall we then say to these things? If God be for us, who can be against us?

'He that spared not his own Son, but delivered him up for us all, how shall he not with him also freely give us all things?

'Who shall lay any thing to the charge of God›s elect? It is God that justifieth.

'Who is he that condemneth? It is Christ that died, yea rather, that is risen again, who is even at the right hand of God, who also maketh intercession for us.

'Who shall separate us from the love of Christ? shall tribulation, or distress, or persecution, or famine, or nakedness, or peril, or sword?

'As it is written, For thy sake we are killed all the day long; we are accounted as sheep for the slaughter.

'Nay, in all these things we are more than conquerors through him that loved us.

'For I am persuaded, that neither death, nor life, nor angels, nor principalities, nor powers, nor things present, nor things to come,

'Nor height, nor depth, nor any other creature, shall be able to separate us from the love of God, which is in Christ Jesus our Lord.'

"So, devil, you have no legal right to remain and I declare you no longer have power over me because God's Word says so. There's power in the Word of God.

"Thank God, I'M FREE. I'M FREE, I'M FREE. PRAISE GOD I'M FREE."

When I was making this declaration, at about halfway through I realized I no longer sensed the power of the devil in the room.

This is not a 'name it and claim it' hyper grace formula. This declaring must be accompanied by a surrendered and committed life. I'm not talking about perfection but a life lived in obedience, open to correction by the Holy Spirit who disciplines and corrects me. There's an authority that comes from genuine intimacy with Jesus.

In Acts 19, where we find the story of the sons of Sceva, we find the results of using a formula without having the genuine authority. There is a group of so-called Jewish exorcists trying to use the name of Jesus. They were professional imitators and they said, "I adjure you by the Jesus whom Paul proclaims." They were challenged by the evil spirit who responded, "Jesus I know, and Paul I know, but who are you?"

They didn't expect the results, but they had stepped into a battle they were not authorized to fight or prepared to fight. Consequently, the evil spirits tore them apart with a beating.

You may have a PhD or a title that you can wave as a banner before man to show your intellectual dominance, but your success in ministry will depend on the life of intimacy, which manifests in victory after victory when doing spiritual warfare.

The acceptance and elevation of man doesn't compare with the favor of God released into our lives at the time of battle because we've taken time not just to know about Him but to KNOW HIM.

CHAPTER 8

CLOSING THE DOOR ON THE DEVIL

Lest Satan should get an advantage of us: for we are not ignorant of his devices.

11Corinthians 2:11

We can allow access for the devil to enter our lives, our homes or our work spaces if we are not mindful of his devices and by not maintaining a disciplined spiritual life. **"Beware of the devil's devices."**

It is my responsibility as a Christian to close all access doors where the enemy can legally step in and build a stronghold. The following is a spiritual checklist of areas that should be monitored frequently to keep myself ACCESS FREE. Attacks will come, and we have the tools to overcome the attack. However, there is no power to overcome without a life that practices holiness and living under the umbrella of protection that is provided when closing all access doors.

An example is: I may declare the Word of God when attacked, but the Holy Spirit will only back me up and empower that declaration when my life is showcasing the disciplines of sanctification and commitment, proceeding out of an intimate relationship with Jesus Christ.

It is my responsibility to watch out for areas where the devil may legally enter. Our lives need to be a NO ACCESS ZONE.

Our character, attitude and actions should hold up a sign for the devil: DO NOT ENTER HERE.

The following are some guidelines to creating a NO ACCESS ZONE FOR THE DEVIL.

1. **Keep a check on your level of surrender and commitment to Christ.** Make a determination that your thoughts, attitudes and actions will reflect the life of Christ.

Romans 12:1 **"I beseech you therefore, brethren, by the mercies of God, that ye present your bodies a living sacrifice, holy, acceptable unto God, which is your reasonable service."**

Memorize Scripture, storing it up so you are ready for the lies of the enemy. You will be ready to declare the Word of God and win the victory. Make frequent deposits of the Word and build up your defensive system. Don't wait to be attacked to open the Bible. In other words, don't let the check reach the bank before you deposit the money. It won't 'work in either the physical or spiritual realm.

Hebrews 4:13 **"The word of God is alive and exerts power and is sharper than any two-edged sword and pierces even to the dividing of soul and spirit, and of joints and their marrow, and is able to discern thoughts and intentions of the heart."**

2. Develop a Life of Praise

Praise is a powerful weapon against the enemy and it is the medicine we need to have a happy heart. When you praise God in every situation, the devil gets hiccups and leaves the room. Praise and worship form a casing around our lives so that even through the trial or attack we feel God's presence and are conscious of His Hand upon us.

Hebrews 12:28-29 "Therefore, since we are receiving a kingdom that cannot be shaken, let us be thankful, and so worship God acceptably with reverence and awe, for our God is a consuming fire."

3. Don't Neglect Prayer

Prayer will fortify your spirit. Speak in tongues and be constantly building yourself up with overcoming spiritual muscles. Prayer creates a radar zone around your life making it difficult for the enemy to penetrate, however he may try.

I Thessalonians 5:17 **"Pray without ceasing."**

4. Practice Positive Confessions

This includes staying away from negative people. Be a person who sees the glass as half full rather than half empty. Positive confession will feed your faith. Negative confessions open access for the enemy. When you hang around people who are talking negative and everything is doom and gloom, when you come away from them you feel soiled and oppressed. A steady diet of that will leave access open for the enemy to plant his negative ideas even more. The pathway is downward after that.

II Corinthians 10:5 **"Casting down imaginations, and every high thing that exalteth itself against the knowledge of God, and bringing into captivity every thought to the obedience of Christ;"**

Guard what you watch and listen to. This includes TV, books, music, movies and Internet.

Just by turning the TV on it's possible to let into your home evil spirits and create a negative atmosphere in your home.

Even some commercials are very offensive to Christian values and principles. It's a good idea to keep the remote close so you can quickly mute or change the channel.

When counseling parents about the behavior in their children, I ask what they watch on TV. The answer reveals the reason for their hyper and rebellious attitudes. Parents need to understand it is their call to set the standard of Christian values in their home. If they fail to do so they will reap the results.

5. **Endeavor to Live in the Spirit and Not in the Flesh. Don't give place to the devil.**

I must choose to live a crucified life by yielding to Christ and obeying His Word, resisting fleshly, carnal, worldly temptations. This type of holy living will close many access doors for the devil.

Ephesians 4:27 **"Beware of his devices."**

Galatians 2:20 **"I am crucified with Christ, nevertheless I live, yet not I but I live by faith in the Son of God who loved me and gave Himself up for me."**

6. **Personal Strife and Toxic Relationships**

We must close these doors by seeking reconciliation, offering restitution where possible. Loving and reaching out to our enemies will close doors where the enemy could do a lot of internal damage. We can overcome evil with good. In this way, we can deny the enemy access to our lives, even though human enemies may abound on every side.

"If thy brother trespass against thee, rebuke him, and if he repents, forgive him."

Luke 17:3

God began convicting me about forgiving my father. I went to him and asked him to forgive me for all the years of hardship I brought on him and my mother through years of self-inflicted acts I had done. At the same time I forgave my dad. Our relationship improved dramatically. Ultimately, God in His mercy granted my father eternal life. I had the privilege of leading him to the Lord on his deathbed. My mother and sister also gave their hearts to the Lord.

In my altar services, when I minister, I often invite people to get rid of unforgiveness so access doors are closed and they have therefore opened the channels whereby God can bless them.

7. Sever All Contact with the Occult or with False Religion

This means horoscope reading and psychic mediums. Get rid of all objects in your house that can be connected to the occult. Also remove all objects including books or magazines

That do not bring glory to God.

"More common in our age of promiscuity and permissiveness is myriads of video games, books and magazines devoted to fantasy; comic books, posters, movies, or music with demonic, violent, or sexual themes: pornography, illegal drugs; sensual art, books or playthings: or a number of other things that are demonic, illegal, immoral or contrary to God's Word."

Chuck Pierce, *Ridding Your Home of Spiritual Darkness.*

Ask the following, according to Peter Wagner

1. Will this open a door to demonic influence?

2. Does this give any appearance of evil?

3. Does this glorify God?

4. By allowing any of these things in our homes we allow a legal right for the enemy to invade our lives in ways that he would otherwise not have. Believers put themselves in dangerous territory when they fail to deal with these potential strongholds that could lead to defeat.

Shut every door

Shut every door, close every window, and seal every place in our lives where the enemy would seek to gain access. We will not be able to move forward until we do this. After we close the doors then we must maintain them shut so we can become candidates for God's blessing and favor. We will then become channels of blessing where God can bless others through our lives.

As the song says, "I'm so glad Jesus set me free. Satan had me bound bur Jesus set me free." I'm so glad that, when I was lost and undone, God reached down His hand for me and by His mercy saved and delivered me. Often I will hear pastors referring to me as the lady with the "needle testimony." I'm quick to make it known that my testimony is truly a story of the mercy of God.

It was certain I would engage in spiritual warfare with the enemy but, thank God, now it would be on a different "battlefield" and I would now have the weapons to fight the good fight of faith and know the enemy's tactics. I was ready through knowing the power of the Word of God, for the battle I would be engaged in as a Christian, the Bible says, "is a good battle." It is a good battle because Jesus Christ has won the battle for us. I John 3:8 **"For this purpose the Son of God was manifested, to destroy the works of the devil."**

As this is a story about the times God stopped me, turned me around, and set me in a new direction, we now continue our journey in Part 11 and see the call of God on my life and then how God, after 27 years of itinerant preaching ministry, again sent me a lifeboat that rescued me from the deep waters of religion re-firing, re-directing and anointing me for greater purposes. With that revival and fresh anointing came a new mandate and vision. God is truly God of a Second Chance.

PART II

A LIFE OF MIRACLES
MY SUPERNATURAL JOURNEY
THE CALL – THE MINISTRY

Acts 20:24

But none of these things move me; nor do I count my life dear to myself,[a] so that I may finish my race with joy, and the ministry which I received from the Lord Jesus, to testify to the gospel of the grace of God.

CHAPTER 9

FROM CHAINS TO MAINE, TO A TASSEL

Study to shew thyself approved unto God, a workman that needeth not to be ashamed, rightly dividing the word of truth. II Timothy 2:15

This was another powerful season of the miracle working power of God- The Call, The Preparation, and 27 years of ministry then God Stops me. What happens after that thank God continues to happen, as it was truly a revelation that gave me a new perspective about God, myself and ministry. It has totally changed my ministry and I continue to be changed.

It was obvious I had a Call of God on my life. With all God had done in my life I knew there was a Divine

Destiny in my future. The Word of God broke the chains and seeing the demonstration of God's power convinced me of the importance of "really" knowing the Bible. The formal study seemed the logical next step. If the Scriptures could be so powerful when quoted achieving my deliverance, what could in-depth knowledge of God's Word bring to my life and others? I could see the fruit of that calling as I seemed to mature in the Lord quickly and was elected to be President of the Youth Group in my church. I knew right away after such a dramatic and wonderful deliverance that I was to give my testimony in churches, conferences or wherever God would open the door.

I began praying, seeking the Lord for direction in Spring of 1971 having been saved in August 1969. Formal education seemed to be the appropriate next step for me. But where would I go? My world view was very limited.

I still battled the oppressive atmosphere in the home. I understood clearly now that the demonic spirits that held me captive for many years were still dominating the atmosphere in the home. Family members argued and there was tension in the air for seemingly no reason at all. Even though I had been dramatically changed experiencing the peace of God. I looked for reasons to be absent from the home because of continual strife and turmoil. I longed for the day I could leave and live on my own. However, that was not possible in a practical sense.

At this time my bedroom became a refuge. I devoured the Bible, Christian books, and commentaries and the entire set of Surgeon's sermons, about 13 volumes. The Lord was my Shield, my Fortress and an ever-present help in time of trouble.

I sought the hope and future that God's Word promised me. As a pilgrim, I sought the spiritual life and felt led to actively plan to go to Bible School. Psalm 119:54 *"Thy statutes have been my songs in the house of my pilgrimage."*

Nancy helped direct me to a good Bible School in Brooklyn Maine, Faith School of Theology.

Up to this point, I was living in Keyport, NJ, a small town near the shore. Maine seemed a remote place like the deserts of Arabia where Paul the Apostle spent time preparing for ministry. However, the winters were not like Arabia! Going to this school was like a spiritual boot camp. Lacking much regiment in my life, the rules and codes seemed rigid at the time. There must have been 613 rules as many as were in the Torah. However, God used this to break and perfect me. I would rely heavily upon Nancy who continued to be my mentor, to clarify things. I would wonder how I could ever become a strong, mature Christian with so many rules but Nancy was always available to straighten out any misunderstandings. She made sure I clearly understood there was nothing I could do in my own ability to earn salvation. Ephesians 2:8 *"For by grace are you saved through faith; and that not of yourselves; it is the gift of God."*

Even when the opposite sex dated, they all met in the dining room, one couple at each table. The house mother walked the room with a ruler and made sure each couple kept the two-foot rule. They were never allowed to be closer than two feet distance from one another. They were allowed occasionally to go out to dinner but were required to have a chaperone with them.

One interesting rule was that boys and girls had activities that always went in the opposite directions. It's a wonder anyone ever got married from the Bible School with all the separate activities and rules.

If it was girl's day to go in the direction of the ocean, then it was boy's day to go towards the town. One day I found myself a "transgressor of the law." On the occasion, I speak of, it was girl's day to go towards the ocean and my roommate and I swam out to an Island and got stuck because the tide went out. The hours rolled into after midnight which was technically now "boys day to the ocean." It was dark and we were AWOL. When we returned, we were muddy and filthy and very embarrassed I might add. The "iron matron" (house mother) was waiting for us. I guess we looked like we had been through "enough" for one night so we were told we would be summoned for an explanation on the following day.

The following day, sure enough, we were called into the office and asked what had happened. We explained but we were not excused so we were consigned to K.P, which translated into having to peel 13 bushels of carrots. To this day, I do not like carrots.

Setting aside all humor I learned the valuable lesson of submitting to authority. God's chain of command must be respected even if we don't agree with all the rules. Romans 13:1 ***"Let every soul be subject unto the higher powers. For there is no power but of God: the powers that be are ordained of God.***

Another important lesson I learned in this school was about trusting God for our needs, Each morning the President would inform the student body of the needs for food for the school. Sometimes He would say "pray because we don't have anything in the kitchen only potatoes for dinner." You can believe a hungry student body took the task seriously to pray for food. Sure enough, as God always did He provided by sending a local farmer with a donation of meat and other foods. Dinnertime would be a time of thanksgiving

The coursework and lectures were far easier; memorizing 100 evangelism scriptures, writing papers on "Why the Word of God was True and learning the foundational doctrines of the faith. I particularly enjoyed homiletics and hermeneutics. I loved to write sermons. Everything was converted into a sermon in my mind. My grades excelled and the President of the school called me into his office one day. He commended me on my excellent grades in homiletics but wanted to impress upon me "the preacher is made from within." At that point, I began to learn a lot about the Potter's Wheel of perfection.

The Lord wants you to know that when the wheel seems to be spinning so fast that you can't get your footing when you feel like you're going to fall, that It is Him, Not the devil. God Himself is forming you and melting you and molding you, sculpting you and HE has HIS hand on you. The Potter's Wheel, although uncomfortable, is a place where the devil cannot access.

So it seemed as though I was in two schools, one for academic learning, and the other for character refinement. I would soon learn the second school would not have graduation just a promotion to a deeper level of refinement of my character and ministry.

God seeks the circumcision not made by human hands, the circumcision of the heart.

Man's righteousness is as filthy rags and these were school regulations and not the marks of maturity that the Bible teaches us about.

God's goal for holy living for us is much more than external conformity to a set of rules. "Spiritual circumcision of the heart" even in the Old Testament means being deeply rooted in Him and having a heart passionate for Him, and driven by a desire to know Him intimately and follow Him in total surrender and commitment. Jeremiah 4:4 ***"Circumcise yourselves to the Lord, and take away the foreskins of your heart, ye men of Judah and inhabitants of Jerusalem: lest my fury come forth like fire, and burn that none can quench it, because of the evil of your doings."***

I learned at an early stage in my ministerial journey of preparation that God was not just going to entrust me with His awesome power and authority and anointing without preparing me on the inside first. Part of that preparation was the crucifixion of self and maturation of strong Christian character and humbling myself. Two things the Holy Spirit kept reminding me:

1. God resists the proud but gives grace to the humble. II Corinthians 12:6-10 "***For though I would desire to glory, I shall not be a fool; for I will say the truth: but now I forbear, lest any man should think of me above that which he seeth me to be, or that he heareth of me.***

And lest I should be exalted above measure through the abundance of the revelations, there was given to me a thorn in the flesh, the messenger of Satan to buffet me, lest I should be exalted above measure.

For this thing, I besought the Lord thrice, that it might depart from me.

And he said unto me, My grace is sufficient for thee: for my strength is made perfect in weakness. Most gladly, therefore, will I rather glory in my infirmities, that the power of Christ may rest upon me.

Therefore, I take pleasure in infirmities, in reproaches, in necessities, in persecutions, in distresses for Christ›s sake: for when I am weak, then am I strong.

2. The greater anointing, we carry, the greater challenges we will have and attacks from the enemy. However, I have the promise of the Word of God, II Corinthians 4:8-9,

II Corinthians 4:17-18, *"For our light affliction, which is but for a moment, worketh for us a far more exceeding and eternal weight of glory; While we look not at the things which are seen, but at the things which are not seen: for the things, which are seen are temporal; but the things which are not seen are eternal."*

I am thankful that God enabled me to obtain excellent grades, and later earn a BA from International Seminary in Florida and a Masters and a Doctorate in Theology at Grace Theological Seminary in Lorus, South Carolina in 2008.

However, the words that the President spoke to me were better understood as I continued my journey in preparing for the ministry, "the preacher is made from within." This school taught me the importance of finding my place, in other words, "my calling."

Through the years, I would find my identity in God revealed. I would also learn how precious the anointing of the Holy Spirit is and how it made the difference between giving a "talk" or a "speech" and preaching a "message" from the heart of God.

In the priesthood of the Old Testament, we see a description of anointing oil. The anointing oil was poured on, it was smeared on, and it was rubbed in. God began to kill some things in my life that would hinder me from having His anointing. The Old Testament teaches us about myrrh. Though myrrh was bitter to the taste when thrown down, stepped on, and crushed it released the most heavenly scent. The more it was battered, bruised and beaten the more powerful the fragrance.

When Jesus came out of the desert He truly had the anointing oil rubbed on Him. He was tested and proven and the anointing rubbed in. Jesus returned in the power of the Spirit to Galilee to begin His full-time ministry as a prophet.

The teachers would frequently talk about the importance of the anointing and its cost.

I began to understand what they really meant was "the anointing will cost you everything."

At this stage of training for my future ministry, I could not know the full impact of what that meant, the anointing costing me everything. But as the journey and the years continued the Holy Spirit taught me the real significance. This was a truth that needed to be "lived out" and experienced rather than learned from a textbook.

CHAPTER 10

TRAIL OF TEARS AND TESTIMONIES AS AN EVANGELIST 1976-1986

"Faithful is he that calleth you, who also will do it. I Thessalonians 5:24

And I thank Christ Jesus our Lord, who hath enabled me, for that he counted me faithful, putting me into the ministry;" I Timothy 1:12

E verything has a beginning, a time of birthing. I wish I knew what I know now when I began my ministerial journey. However, chapters in this book would not be necessary if I bypassed all the lessons and jumped to perfection. There would be no lessons to teach that were products of trials and tribulations spinning on the potter's wheel.

Then, how could I help or minister to others? If it were not for the piercing and crucifying of the Word of God in my life I would not have the power of His precious Holy Spirit enabling me to live an overcomer's life and minister under the anointing. Sometimes I felt that I would never arrive, but my mentor reminded me when I would get discouraged that God was making something beautiful out of my life.

As the Potter, He molds us, then puts us into the fire to be hardened and made useful. When the potter takes the vessel out, after a while, He thumps on it listening for the sound it produces. He listens for a certain sound. If the sound is cold and hard, He puts it back in the fire. He repeats this process until He hears the beautiful ringing sound. Only when it has that beautiful ring, and it sings in the fire is it ready to be used for God's glory. Throughout my ministry, I had to keep reminding myself to "sing in the fire."

As a student in college preparing for the ministry I was earnestly praying about what ministry I was to have. "Lord, what do you want me to do?" The Lord began to put a passion in my heart to preach.

I had a vision of a church and I was preaching. As the Word of God left my lips it would be converted into flames of fire landing on people in the congregation and breaking chains of bondage. To this day, I remember this vision vividly.

I prayed and asked God to open a door on one of the teams for outside ministry to have an opening for me to fill as the preacher for the team. I wanted a confirmation to the "call of God" I was sensing.

Each weekend the students from college were sent out in teams for ministry. One Sunday as I was part of an evangelistic team ministering in a church not far from the school, I was assigned to preach and include my testimony in the message. When we arrived at the church I was amazed as I looked at the church. It was the same color and size as the one in my vision. When we went inside I definitely identified it as the one in my vision. My nervousness was transformed into excitement as I again pictured the Word going forth and the flames of fire breaking chains. I felt a boldness come upon me and the Scripture came to my mind *"The Spirit of the Lord God is upon Me because the Lord hath anointed Me to preach good tidings unto the meek. He hath sent me to bind up the brokenhearted, to proclaim liberty to the captives, and the opening of the prison to them that are bound."* Isaiah 61:1

The ministry team ministered to people who responded to the altar call and people were saved and delivered. We gave God all the honor, praise and the glory as we traveled back to a college campus that day. I pondered in my heart the events of the day and I accepted God's call to preach. I asked the Lord for another confirmation as we were getting ready for the two-month winter break; an invitation to preach at my local church. The first Sunday I was back the pastor invited me to minister every other Sunday night during the two-month break and on the alternate Sunday preach at the Rest Home. I was excited: I had an assignment and another confirmation. I wasn't too nervous because my mentor, Nancy would be there in the congregation praying for me.

In the beginning of my years preaching I was trying to find out "who I was." I had listened to many great preachers and I would try to copy their style. I use to be self-conscious of my "manly," voice. I tried to make it sound more feminine but to no avail. I felt "out of place" because of my deep voice and I also felt like I was in a man's world because in 1960's 70's the church was still overcoming the prejudice against women preachers. My friends sent me gifts of lacy and dainty style blouses to wear under my tailored suits. I remember putting a dainty, lacy type blouse on while dressing to go preach one night and I only had it on for about 30 minutes and looked into the mirror and I took it off and put something else on because the lace was not my style. I settled that issue that night and decided again, the best person I can be is me. If I have a powerful anointing anyway nobody is going to be paying attention to my non-frilly attire. I was actually glad I had a deep and powerful voice when I preached in Puerto Rico in an outside crusade and the power went out but I could keep on preaching with my "manly" voice.

After looking silly and making mistakes, trying to be somebody I was not, I decided the best person I could be was me. Nancy told me one day at her "mentoring table," "Holly, stop trying so hard, just be you." She assured me that if I would pray and wait on God before I ministered, the Holy Spirit would perfect the delivery of my message. I learned that God doesn't want to change me into being somebody else He wants to use the person and personality that He made. Thank God we're not all the same, as is true in the natural. There are different sizes, colors, shapes, personalities all over the world in the Body of Christ.

When I was in college I was, as usual, the perfectionist I had always been. I would cry over getting a grade of a "B." It took me a while to learn the success of my message was not dependent on my perfection but on the anointing of the Holy Spirit.

Between the years of 1969 through 1976, I traveled throughout the Northeast and went to California also. I traveled to the mid-west and as far south as Florida on the East coast. Having been freshly delivered from the hand of the devil my testimony was very popular. The services were very powerful as people were saved and delivered at the altar. It was so exciting to see people being set free from the very power that had held me captive. Now through the power of the Word of God, I was an instrument in the hand of God to set others free. I would leave every service with an excitement and a profound gratitude that now instead of running from the devil he was running from me when I put him in his place through the Word of God.

One day I met someone and we began to have fellowship together and she invited me to go with her to a Spanish church. Although her father was a pastor in an English- speaking church they ministered in Spanish churches also. They invited me to give my testimony with a translator. This was my first time to ever go to a Spanish church. After I ministered in that church with a translator, I was invited to other Spanish churches. I received many more invitations in Spanish churches, always using a translator. Never did I think that God would lead me into a Bi-lingual ministry full time in the future. I kept reasoning with God as if He didn't know, that I was American and my language was English. I soon learned that God doesn't use our reasoning to help in His decisions. It seemed that God was giving me some big lessons to learn early in my ministry. I soon would realize this was God's way of drawing me into a new ministry with new people. I was excited but also moving ahead cautiously.

One lesson I learned in my early days of ministry was how to know God's will. One thing that helped me discern God's will was the way I prayed. I learned that it was important to bring my mind to a place of neutrality so God could speak to me and lead me. Sometimes we are so convinced of the way we want to go or what we want to do that we try to convince God through prayer to allow us to do what we prefer, rather than asking God what He really wants us to do. When the human emotion of personal preferences enters in, the real picture of God's will can be obscured. When God gives us the direction we seek, we need to act on it. It is God's responsibility to show us His will for our life and our responsibility to nurture His calling. ***"For my thoughts are not your thoughts, neither are your ways my ways, saith the Lord. For*** *as the heavens are higher than the earth, so are my ways higher than your ways, and my thoughts than your thoughts."* Isaiah 55:8-9

Paul said that God had separated him from his mother's womb and called him by His grace *"But when it pleased God, who separated me from my mother's womb and called me by his grace."* Galatians 1:15 It was in the plan of God for Paul to be a minister of the Gospel before he was ever born. God didn't evaluate his gifts and talents and then decide He could use him. So, if you only look at what you're good at to determine your purpose, you may totally miss it. God will undoubtedly use your gifts and talents. They come from Him anyway. You may have a gift to sell and you are working as a professional salesperson. That does not mean that the call of God could not be upon your life. Maybe God would use your selling ability to evangelize. God can also take someone that has no ability to sell in the natural but He can enable them upon calling them.

Many people in the church are doing good works, but that doesn't necessarily mean they're walking in God's purpose for their lives. Not everything that is good is God. Understanding the way God works will enable us to know His will in our lives.

I finally laid aside my rationalizations about why I didn't qualify for Spanish ministry and surrendered to the will of God. His peace filled my heart and even though I did not know where the road would lead to the Spanish opportunities I knew I was on the right road, going in the right direction because God was leading. When the opportunities came to preach in a Spanish church I went with the confidence that God knew what He was doing in my life and ministry even if I didn't understand. That kind of obedience required faith and so the process of perfecting me went to the next level.

I was invited to hold a crusade in a Church in South Jersey. This was an English-speaking church. The services were very powerful and people were changed in the Presence of God night after night as people waited until late in the night around the altar. I was very excited especially since I was just beginning to hold crusades. The church was so impacted by my Testimony they asked me to give it several nights and every time people would be mightily changed by the power of God. As a young minister, I was surprised to see all of this happening. I was also excited wondering what the future held. I would return home late into the night and upon lying on my bed to rest I could not contain my tears of gratitude and humility before the Lord and I gave God all the glory and the honor and the praise.

The pastor asked me to assume the role as Associate Pastor and stay and work with him and his wife. I prayed about it and when the crusade was over I accepted the position. After fulfilling the licensing requirements, I became a minister with the Church of

God, headquarters in Cleveland, Tennessee. In this position, I learned many invaluable lessons in ministry. This assignment was truly a proving ground and after about a year I realized how much I did not know. However, I could see how every opportunity God gave me had a dual purpose. It was for me to minister to the people in whatever capacity but God also would use that position to teach me so many new lessons, weaving new threads into my ministerial profile defining the characteristics of my ministry in the future.

I returned to the New York, Connecticut and Pennsylvania region and enjoyed many wonderful special services featuring my Testimony and longer meetings where I had crusades and saw many deliverances and healings. I did this for several years, traveling throughout mainly the Northeast of the US. I was still battling a negative environment in my home so I was happy to stay away as long as possible. I enjoyed staying with many wonderful people They ministered to my need for a place to stay as I ministered throughout the churches and I ministered to them as I stayed in their homes.

I was asked to go to a convention in Puerto Rico that the Church of God was having in 1977. This was a very interesting trip and a springboard to future opportunities. I was invited to stay in Puerto Rico after the convention and give my testimony throughout the Island. The Pastor hosting my stay would send a car to the home where I was staying to take me to all the engagements to preach.

I had the opportunity to see a lot of Puerto Rico. I had a translator who traveled with me who was provided by the hosting pastor. They took me to churches in the mountains and in the cities. The services were very powerful and God moved mightily. They didn't want me to leave but I had to. I promised to return and I did in the early eighties and I lived there for about a year and a half.

I especially enjoyed ministering at a rehabilitation center for addicts. I loved sharing with others who were in bondage how I was living proof of the delivering power of Jesus Christ. So many of them looked as if they were in deep bondage and seeking to come out of it. I could feel their pain and suffering as I looked into their faces and passionately related to them that though it seemed like they were on a dead-end street there was hope and His name is Jesus Christ.

My month in Puerto Rico was very enjoyable. I learned to love eating the way they cooked Rice and beans, fried green banana with garlic and Spanish dishes, such as stew and churrasco. We Americans just can't cook those rice and beans like the Spanish folks. Hmm!

Before I left Puerto Rico I met a Pastor who invited me to minister in the churches in the Dominican Republic. He was assistant to the Superintendent in the Dominican Republic. I told him I would pray about it and let him know. As I continued my Evangelistic travels God kept nudging me about contacting him. I wrote him a letter and accepted the invitation. I never realized that the very opportunity I was putting off would be a plan-changer for the vision of future ministry. I had a translator who traveled with me and I went to many different churches. During one of my Crusades, my translator told me he would be returning to the United States and wouldn't be able to continue translating for me. We had seen many salvations, healings, and deliverances but at this time I was beginning to feel ill because of intestinal problems due to food and water changes.

The thought occurred to me that maybe I was finished and this would be an appropriate time to return to the United States and take some time to get better. I had been there for six months anyway and I could come back at a future date. I had lost 30lbs and was looking a bit sickly. However, the Holy Spirit did not give me a release to leave the country. I prayed and asked God if I didn't speak the language or have an interpreter what was I going to do. The Lord said to me "All things are possible if you can believe. Go preach I am with you." That night when I went to church to preach we were in the middle of a crusade and I tried to tell pastor I couldn't preach in Spanish. I expected God would send a translator but that didn't happen. God came Himself. I was handed the microphone and God gave me the supernatural ability to preach for the very first time in Spanish. Everyone was amazed, including me! God was fulfilling His Word where Jesus said in Mark 9:23, "If thou canst believe all things are possible to him that believeth."

The crusade catapulted into a great success as there was great interest to see the woman who started the crusade in English and was ending it in Spanish. God drew the crowds and people were touched nightly by the anointing of the Holy Spirit Who was present to heal and deliver. After receiving such a miracle of enabling from the Lord I was ready to accept fully God's call for me to expand my ministry to Spanish-speaking peoples.

Now I understand why God did not release me to leave the country even though I was so sick. He had a purpose to fulfill. After the storm, there was a beautiful rainbow of a miracle from God. After several weeks of sickness and suffering little did I know that the end of the story had such a beautiful ending. Many times, I thought I'd die there feeling so sick but something had me press forward. When I recall the perseverance during those hard times, it always brings a sweetness, the glory of God comes with a cost. However, we are reminded what the Scripture says about suffering and it gives us hope, ***"For I reckon that the sufferings of this present time are not worthy to be compared with the glory which shall be revealed in us."*** Romans 8:18

"That the trial of your faith, being much more precious than of gold that perisheth, though it be tried with fire, might be found unto praise and honor and glory at the appearing of Jesus Christ:" I Peter 1:7

During these times, I learned about being faithful to God and His call He had placed on my life. God's grace was truly sufficient and on this trail of tears, I learned total dependence on the Lord. God told me to "use the vocabulary He gave me and He would increase it every time I ministered. "He made my mind like a computer with Spanish so to speak. I would only have to see or hear something once to have it indelibly printed on my mind. It required an act of faith every time I preached as I had to believe that even though I would have a few notes that I would need the rest of the vocabulary for the completion of the preaching and prophetic words I would speak to the people. God increased my vocabulary inasmuch as I can now read an entire book and write on a non-professional level. When I speak and minister in Spanish I always feel that same anointing that came upon me the very first time God performed the miracle.

I've hit a few bumps in the road probably when doubt or fear tried to take control. One time in a crusade I was having an altar service after the preaching I started calling the "Caballos" instead of the "Caballeros" however they came to the altar. I was calling the horses instead of the men. On another occasion when gathered with a few lady friends for some reason I said I felt "embarazada" meaning I feel "embarrassed." I was unintentionally saying I was pregnant instead of embarrassed. I never made those mistakes again. I have learned to laugh at myself and laugh at the humorous way I must look to our Spanish friends when they see a "gringa" killing their language. However, through the years, I've come a long way.

I was also honored to have been asked to be the speaker for the Women' National Convention of the

Church of God. The Dominican Republic has a very special place in my heart being the place God gave me Spanish. I have gone back there several times to minister since that time.

CHAPTER 11

GOD'S ANSWER TO WHAT COULD HAVE BEEN A LONELY ROAD MY ARMORBEARER, AND BEST FRIEND LOIS DIETRICH -1987

"Do All that you have in mind," his armor-bearer said. "Go ahead;

I am with you heart and soul."

I Samuel 14:7

WOW, God cares about the littlest details in our lives.

Many have asked me along my ministerial journey if I am married. I am not married but God has blessed me tremendously. I had the opportunity to marry and of course, I prayed and the Lord said although He would permit me to marry I would not have the same ministry as I would if I remained single. I decided to remain single but I asked the Lord to send someone like a sister or an associate in ministry. This is by no means an indictment on marriage. This was just not God's will for me.

My ministry led me to a church where Lois was a member. I preached and was invited to have a crusade and God moved mightily. To God be the glory. After ministering frequently at this church I was asked to come on staff. I was taking people out to visit in the afternoons and asked for volunteers. Lois raised her hand and said she would be available every day after she was done teaching school. We went out visiting together quite often and then developed a friendship. We enjoyed ministering together and we also enjoyed each other's company.

There were changes in plans with the senior pastor and I was going back into my Evangelistic ministry.

I asked Lois if she wanted to visit a Spanish church since a big part of my ministry was in Spanish. She went with me and she embraced the Spanish culture amazingly and she said "yes" when I wanted her to continue with me and become my associate. Lois loved Spanish services. As a matter of fact, she loved everything Spanish: the people, the form of expression, the food, the cultures even as they varied in different countries.

I had changed over to be Licensed Minister with Spanish District and was ordained in 1992 in the Assemblies of God. I asked Lois to pursue credentialing also. She told me this was an answer to prayer she had always prayed that she could work full-time for the Lord. Since her children had grown up and had families of their own she had that liberty especially since her husband granted his approval. When God is in something He puts everything in order. It's only doing things God's way that we can expect His blessing on what we are doing.

Everything seemed to be in order, except one thing. To buy into Lois' retirement, getting credit for years she taught outside NJ, she needed $15,000. Their house needed to be sold at a certain price so she could downsize and pay the $15,000. A Miracle occurred while we were at Mahanaim for Lois' licensing the house was sold. Against all odds. The house needed repair on a septic system. God sent a contractor who bought it and for him, those repairs were not major. The price was paid to meet every need to the penny.

Every ministry needs a "Lois." She became my Armor bearer y associate and best friend. It was just like having a sister. Lois said, "God told me to take care of you." Lois has been fulfilling her calling now for more than thirty years and still counting. She is a wonderful friend also. God gave me the very best, the cream of the crop. Lois has an anointing to serve and help and she does it loyally and sacrificially. She counsels me and comforts me in a time of need. She has a gentle and sweet personality and people love her to minister her encouraging words either at the altar or after service. She has a way of winning peoples' confidence with her cheery attitude and bright smile. She is a wonderful complement to my personality.

Because of my type ministry God has given me a bold voice and authority that comes with leadership qualities. We complement each other and work well together making a great team for the glory of God. God truly answered my prayer for someone to be my associate and covenant partner by giving me, Lois. Not only do we work well together but we both enjoy life together apart from ministry. We laugh together and cry together and bear one another's burdens.

I'm reminded of how God supported friendships in the Bible. He even said it was not good for man to be alone. Jonathan and David come to my mind as being a classic example of a partnership which was also a close friendship. 1 Samuel 18 describes their friendship: ***"As soon as he had finished speaking to Saul, the soul of Jonathan was knit to the soul of David, and Jonathan loved him as his own soul."***

Jonathan sacrificed for David, stripping himself of the items which were symbolic of his power and position, and giving them to him. Jonathan was also with resolute determination to be loyal to David, warning him of King Saul's treachery and intent to kill him.

Elijah was the prophet of Israel, who called down the fires of heaven, defeating the prophets of Baal, and the man who caused a drought in Israel for three years through prayer. To assist him fulfill his ministry, God saw fit to send Elijah a friend and eventual successor, the younger Elisha. Elisha attaches himself to Elijah, insisting that he not leave him in 2 Kings 2:2. Responding to Elijah's declaration that he was leaving for Bethel, Elisha exclaims, ***"As the Lord lives, and as you yourself live, I will not leave you."*** Elisha was absolutely devoted to his friend, to his mentor.

CHAPTER 12

A DESIRE TO BIRTH SOMETHING, THE CALL TO MISSIONS 1991

And a vision appeared to Paul in the night: a man of Macedonia was standing there, urging him and saying, "Come over to Macedonia and help us." Acts16:9

Up to this point, I was basically a traveling evangelist and I held services and crusades in the United States traveling in the Northeast, and to California before Lois joined the ministry. I had also held crusades in Puerto Rico and the Dominican Republic

At this time, I formed a Board of Directors and incorporated my ministry under the name HOLLY NOE

MINISTRIES but still remaining Ordained minister with the Assemblies of God. Having spoken with General Counsel headquarters they advised me that evangelists who desired to pursue non-profit status needed to incorporate independently. As President and Founder of the ministry, I personally would be affiliated with the Assemblies of God. This would be the best way to receive donations from partners and branch out into different areas of ministry, as I was anticipating doing.

A time came that Lois and I decided to expand our Evangelistic ministry to have a large concentration in mission work after God burdened me for missions as He put a desire in me and Lois to birth something. We prayed for God to lead us how to start making a difference in the arena of missions. We went to our Director of Missions, Dr. Valdez and we shared our burden. He suggested we go to missionaries already on the field and help them. After we began helping the missionaries he affectionately called us "God's angels to the missionaries." Looking back over the years I'm amazed how God has taken that desire and through the years developed it into a dream that is still being fulfilled. This was a lesson to show us how God walks us through every step to fulfill a dream. Only God knows how to work with each person to draw out the gifts and talents and even give that person more abilities to fulfill the mandate. Truly His calling is His enabling. I might note here that God is not in a hurry to accomplish His eternal purposes with us.

Our very first trip was to Guatemala to work with Pastors Richard & Lupita Sherman. They had only been there getting set up and exploring their field of labor a short period of time. We spent six weeks traveling with them and preaching throughout the country. Eventually, we arrived in Livingston where they would set up a house and start services next door. As we traveled we stayed in the very simple houses of pastors and members of churches. We had to learn everything through experience but such lessons in hygiene and how to keep from getting sick prepared us for the ministry we would have in later years when we would take groups on Mission Trips. It was like a six-week boot camp that shook up our American attitudes towards comfort and materialism.

I remember one day the dear sister who brought us to what was to be our "washroom" and said she would heat the water. She plugged one end into the socket and on the other end was a cord with wires exposed and when she rubbed it together she got some sparks. We both came from middle-class homes and were not used to heating up water with an electric wire When I saw the sparks I politely said, thank you but no thank you. We were fearful of being electrocuted. The bathroom was in the form of an outhouse. We tried not to have to go there because of the stench.

Living in simple dwellings was not as much a problem

as the lack of cleanliness. We were sick with diarrhea often, a problem which was made even more difficult without much toilet paper. If you were in a public place there was a woman collecting a quarter at the bathroom door for a very small piece of paper. We learned to travel with toilet paper. On the long roads to get to where we had to minister there were no decent bathrooms. There were times we found ourselves in a field by the roadside. I ministered at a church in the mountain and asked where the bathroom was and they pointed to a cornfield in the distance on the side of a mountain. Both Lois and I walked a distance to get to the cornfield to an imaginary bathroom and you can figure out the rest of that story.

One night after a long day of traveling we were shown to the room where we would spend the night. It was a room on the outside of the house and the door had no lock. The bathroom was the outhouse. The beds were home-made with very thin mattresses. We got ready for bed and after getting into bed and turning out the lights we heard a loud noise which sounded like an animal. We thought it was coming from under the bed. I said to Lois, "Did you hear that? Look under the beds. "Lois said, "I'm not going to look under there.". We prayed and worshiped and eventually fell asleep. In the morning, Lois opened the door to the bedroom and out from under Lois' bed flew a little colorful parrot. It was a household pet named Willie we were told.

One night we were shown to the room where we would sleep. The beds were wooden with a mat type covering for a mattress. It wasn't a "perfect sleeper" and it was difficult on my back. At that time in Guatemala, the roads were much worse than they are now. When we traveled on our first trip the roads would have large gaping holes that would appear out of nowhere. We always had to keep supplies of purified bottled water with us because the water is contaminated. The food needed to be prepared in a way to cleanse it of impurities from hanging in the open-air market where flies infested it. Since that time, we learned from people in Guatemala who were educated to the preparing of food so it would not make us sick. Those lessons were valuable to our present work in taking groups and keeping them safe. Guatemala now has improved over the last 25 years so that there has been a vast modernization in each area that was a threat to our well-being.

We went to Entre Rios to hold a crusade and stayed in the pastor's home. We did a joint crusade for adults and children. The power of God was manifested and there was much fruit for the glory of God. There were 128 children saved in that crusade and we give God all the glory and honor. However, the living conditions in this place were the worse we experienced. The house had dirt floors and the room where we slept had two beds with makeshift mattresses. Rats ran throughout the house at night. To use the bathroom at night we had to travel through the house and go outside across the yard to the outhouse. In the daytime, there were chickens and a pig in the living room. In the morning, Lois went out to see the ladies making tortillas and she came back to the bedroom with an upsetting report: She said, "the pig is eating from the bucket of corn the ladies are using to make the tortillas." I decided we wouldn't be eating any more tortillas. However, when the Presence and power of God came down in the services it was worth it all. We were strengthened to keep going on and not give up. We learned about "pressing on" and "persevering." It was important to maintain the victory that we kept our eyes on the Lord and the reason we were there.

When Pastor Rich decided to set up housekeeping in Livingston we had a crusade and he began to lay the groundwork involved in starting a new work. Since this is a seaport town we were blessed with eating at an excellent seafood restaurant that Pastor Rich took us to. However, we had to take a very rough ride in a boat bouncing through rough waters sometimes to go from Puerto Barrios to Livingston. It was a long walk up the hill to his future home. We invested the funds we brought in helping him with furnishing the house and building a structure on the side of his house to provide a place to start services. We thank God, we could help him in his beginning days to get started. After that time, he went on to build a school and a more appropriate place for services and disciple and train a staff of teachers and preachers. His work in Livingston stands today as a testimony to his diligence and obedience to God's call. I was an eyewitness to some of what he and his wife went through in the way of trials and tribulations. However, they always "pressed on to the mark of the high calling in Christ Jesus." They were examples of perseverance and longsuffering.

Towards the end of our experience in Guatemala, Pastor Rich took us to San Juan Chamelco where we met a fellow minister he knew well, Pastor Moses Moran. We ministered in his church and he shared with us his vision to build a school with complete licensure. I looked at a heap of sand and rock and he said to me, "we have been praying for a missionary to help us with this project and I believe God has sent you here for that purpose." I made a promise to help with some offerings but told him I didn't feel that I was "his missionary." I did promise to pray. At that point, we were physically worn out from the rigors of the journey and we were looking forward to going home and not even thinking about returning to Guatemala.

I remembered I had asked the Lord to use us to birth something. But this is a gigantic project I thought. I should have known by now that when you ask God to birth something and use you He always gives you a vision that is much bigger than you are able to fulfill. He does that for a reason: "in our weakness, His strength is made perfect." The glory and honor of the completed project are for Him. I give God all the glory and honor for His marvelous works. I had no idea what God had in mind and would be revealed at a later time. As I look back now over more than 20 years of mission work in Guatemala I can truly say surely it was the Lord who has brought us this far. I feel like there is no greater position to fill but to be a servant of God and be led by Him to work in His kingdom. Some people get excited about one day in heaven walking on streets of gold. What excites me is to hear God say to me "Well done, good and faithful servant."

"Not that we are competent in ourselves to claim anything for ourselves, but our competence comes from God." II Corinthians 3:5 (NIV)

I felt sorry for Pastor Rich. He certainly had a lot on his plate. Even though he was going through a difficult time himself he always looked for opportunities to bless us. He was just settling into a new field of labor. His wife was pregnant and we had to travel in a pick-up truck with Lois and Lupita riding in the back. Despite the contrary circumstances, they provided the very best they had available to them to host us. At the end of a long season of traveling Pastor Rich said he was taking us to preach in the city and to meet a friend of his. He said we were going to be blessed. After ministering in the church where we were invited we were taken to a wealthy lady's home in a very upscale part of Guatemala City. She treated us like royalty and we all enjoyed a time of rest and refreshing. God always provides a way of escape during the trial. ***"But God is faithful; He will not suffer you to be tempted beyond that which ye are able to bear, but with the temptation will also make a way to escape, that ye may be able to bear it."*** 1Corinthians 10:13

Thru each circumstance that was hard God reminded

me of a Scripture and helped us to worship and not complain. We realized through all the lack of comfort and our reaction to it that we needed to die to self even more. So, we submitted and asked God for grace. We know that God was working in us a greater purpose and showing us that the typical American ideology of comfort and the "it's all about me" attitude would not work here on the mission field. We left Guatemala at that time with a greater appreciation for our blessings. We had no idea what God had in store for future ministry in Guatemala but it was big. For now, though we were just being perfected and prepared. God was teaching us to be willing to do whatever He wants us and calls us to do. We may think in our human minds that is too hard but God will never ask us to do anything that is too hard for us without giving us the grace where we find our sufficiency. When God sees our obedience and readiness to do what He asks He makes us fruitful giving us the ability and the anointing. The more we recognize our frailty and inability the more anointing and power God pours into our lives.

We were introduced to the Yucatan, Mexico through Pastor Rich and Lupita. We visited there together with them and had a very enjoyable trip. We preached there and enjoyed the city of Merida very much. The services were full of the power of God and many were saved and touched with the presence of the Holy Spirit. A couple years later we were invited back to the Yucatan Peninsula by Rev. Blanca, the Superintendent of the Assemblies of God in that region. We were very honored that he prepared a 10-day ministerial agenda throughout the region.

There are a couple of experiences that stand out in my mind. We arrived in a place called Popolnah, Mexico. The church was packed, standing room only. I gave my testimony and the altar was filled with people seeking deliverance from many different types of bondage. We left the service that night feeling that the Lord had His way and many were changed by the power of God. Something very strange occurred there though. The people were all staring out both Lois and myself. They didn't take their eyes off us. I asked the pastor after the service why everyone was staring at us. We were quite amused at his answer. He said they were fascinated with our blue eyes since they had never seen anyone with blue eyes before.

At the house, where we stayed there was another interesting and trying experience. The hardest part was dealing with the uncleanliness and the unsanitary conditions with the food and bacteria growing on it which causes illness. Each day they would serve chicken and leave the leftovers out sitting on the stove all night in the hot weather. They would eat that same chicken the next day and that was a concern to us. We prayed they would not serve it to us but they would get a fresh chicken. God, in His mercy, answered our prayers and each morning we saw the man of the house come home with a fresh chicken. Each night we were ministering and God kept us and worked many such miracles to overcome the lack of sanitary conditions. However, I thank God for all these experiences as it was God's classroom for when we would return to the mission field and bring groups and God taught us how to keep them healthy. We also met people in our travels throughout Guatemala that were more educated on this subject and they shared with us the methods they use for the preparation of food to ensure its safety.

We were told a brother from the church was giving us the use of his condo right on the waterfront in the Yucatan. We were excited for a time of refreshing. The first night we were surprised when the beds were full of sand and we had to sleep on them. When Lois got up she yelled like a scared person. I went to see what had happened and I saw these giant size cockroaches literally taking over the living room. I took a big rocking chair and Lois sprayed them with hairspray first and then I killed them with the chair. It was no better outside on the beach. It was littered with garbage and crawling things that sort of killed our desire to enjoy the ocean. Our first six weeks in Guatemala and our Evangelistic journey in Mexico must have been God's boot camp for us because since that time we never went through those types of trials again.

The last Crusade which was part of the Yucatan tour was held in Cozumel. The services were amazingly favored with the awesome Presence of God. People were saved and healed and God was glorified. That's what it's all about anyway.

Pastor Valdez asked us to go to Honduras to help Mario Fumero so we extended our borders to Honduras. We enjoyed working with Mario Fumero as he was a seasoned man of God having been on the mission field many years and had even gained favor with the president of the country at one point. The best way to learn something is to watch and walk beside someone who has already done the job and has had success in doing it. His center for Rehabilitation is well known in Honduras and he has raised up many future ministers. I preached in several of his works and traveled throughout the region. We ministered at a rehabilitation center bringing my testimony which was very powerful to the young men that were fighting drug addiction. We invested funds that we brought with us to help the center where there were a great number of needs at that time.

CHAPTER 13

OPEN DOORS OR OPEN HEAVEN

As the deer pants for the water brooks,
So my soul pants for You, O God.
[2] My soul thirsts for God, for the living God…
Psalm 42:1,2

LOIS' INSATIABLE HUNGER

While I was studying for my theological degrees we would go to the Theological Seminary library and Lois would read books about the old-time revivalists while I worked on my papers. Lois was reading books by Charles Finney, Smith Wigglesworth, John Wesley and George Whitefield. I carried books on Theology, and Lois carried books on revival. After receiving my Masters in Theology and then several years later a Doctorate in Theology I would learn intellectual knowledge about God is vastly different than experiential knowledge. As Daniel said, they that do know their God shall do great exploits. However intimate relationship would lead to His revival power.

Many days I would find Lois with a box of tissues reading the books by the revivalists with tears and she said to me, "I don't see these things happening in our ministry, what's wrong."? My response to Lois was "I do my job, preaching and the rest is up to God."

I was satisfied with preaching and I believed in supernatural power, however, I didn't understand that I had to run after His Presence. But I would learn that Presence must precede methodology. I was following the normal route to success for ministers. I thought that would help my ministry. Lois's route was pursuing God, my method would open doors her pursuit would open heaven.

I would find that years of theological study couldn't produce the fruit of knowing Him and abiding in the vine. The sap of His Presence brings the fruit of holiness and power.

It seemed that Lois' goal now was more of God. She was convinced that there was more and she was going after Him. I know that God sent her to be an agent of change and transformation in my life and ministry. God surely brought me a partner and a friend but He had an even greater purpose to fulfill.

"My goal is GOD HIMSELF. Not joy, not peace, not even blessing but HIMSELF...my GOD." Leonard Ravenhill

Hunger and thirst are the two main ingredients in a person's pursuit of God.

In Matthew 5:6, Jesus tells us,

*Blessed are those who **hunger and thirst** for righteousness, for **they will be filled**."*

God wants to fill us more than we want to be filled. When we show the least amount of hunger towards Him He comes to us and fills us and it just makes us hungry for more.

There were great revivals throughout history that have been birthed out of the hunger and thirst of a few consecrated individuals. John Wesley, the forefront revivalist of the First Great Awakening of the 1700s, stated, *If you want to see revival, get on fire for God, and people will come to see you burn."*

You don't need a crowd of people to move God's hand. One person's persistent hunger for God can usher in His manifest presence.

C.S. Lewis wrote in The Weight of Glory, «We are far too easily pleased. That, in the end, is the reason we do not pray more than we do. Nothing less than infinite joy is offered us in God's kingdom of light. He has promised that we will one day shine like the sun in that kingdom (Matthew 13:43).»

«We have become satisfied with the mere church, mere religious exertion, mere numbers, and buildings—the things we can do. There is nothing wrong with these things, but they are no more than foam left by the surf on the ocean of God's glory and goodness.» [Ben Patterson, Deepening Your Conversation With God, 171.]

The hand of God wouldn't allow Lois to rest. Desperation and discontentment grew more and more especially after hearing reports about the outpouring of the Holy Spirit in the Brownsville Revival. The same Holy Spirit that set ministries on fire like Wesley and Wigglesworth were setting a church on fire in Pensacola Florida. Lois was determined to go. I told her, I would only go to Brownsville if we were in the area because of a preaching engagement. Well, the day finally came that we would be in Florida and Lois showed me the map and how the Brownsville Assembly of God where the Revival was could easily be a stop for us on our way back home. I planned one day to be there. I was so sorry after we got there that I only configured one day into our schedule. Since that time I've learned much about Divine appointments and I decided I'd rather be on God's calendar than for me to schedule God into my agenda.

When we arrived at Brownsville Assembly of God we saw the long line of people and we learned that they had been in line since 4 AM for the service beginning at 7 PM. I said to Lois, "What is going on here, I've never seen people lining up like this for a church service.?" However, I would learn later this was not any ordinary church service as I knew it. Whap, the Holy Spirit hit me like a high-speed snowball in the car. I wept and began to repent and I said to the Lord, "forgive me for my resistance and stubbornness and do anything you want to in my life, I surrender." I was already two years behind Lois as far as being hungry for more but I was like a freight train, slow getting started but high speed from now on. It didn't take long to catch up once I tasted what was going on in these meetings.

We got in line with hundreds of others and were amazed at the testimonies people were sharing about the services they had already experienced. God was doing supernatural things in their lives and you could see the excitement and the joyful anticipation of what they were expecting for that night. We heard security come over the loud speaker directing us to file in a single line, leave your backpacks, large purses, umbrellas and the announcement went on with a long list of requirements and instructions. I realized the spiritual implications to these instructions. I was enlisting in revival boot camp, I just had to leave my baggage at the door.

If you want revival you too must leave your baggage at the door. Even if you can't leave all your baggage the Holy Spirit is the most gracious and effective porter, He's the Servant in the Godhead, the Teacher, and the Converter. It is easy to avoid conviction of sin, for the Spirit's voice is gentle. Only those who are eager to be convicted will hear His voice, and they only will be eager because they hunger for the Lord and know that this is the only way by which they will be freed from the things that separate them from Him.

The Bible story of Naaman not being willing to obey the prophet's word is a good illustration of resistance of the very thing that opens the portals of blessing on our lives. Naaman was instructed to go to the Jordan and wash seven times. He would have done anything else but that. That would mean stripping and an extent of his leprosy being seen. He finally yielded to the gentle pleas of his servants, and his flesh came again like the flesh of a child. See (2 Kings 5:13-14)

The door of repentance and obedience had to be opened to go into the next room where God had Naaman's miracle. How many miracles and blessings are we missing out on because of not recognizing our need for repentance and obedience.

INSIDE THE CHURCH

Now we are inside the church, people were running down the aisles to get a seat. In a matter of minutes the entire church, balcony, and overflow rooms in the main building were filled and the overflow rooms were also filled and the educational building which was located across the street.

Lindell Cooley began to lead worship. In a few minutes, the sanctuary was not only filled with people that were hungry for God but it was filled with an awesome Presence of God more powerful than I had ever felt in my entire Christian life

People came by busloads. There were international visitors on a regular basis. The testimonies were breathtaking, Marriages restored, addictions are broken, bodies healed and worn out backslidden pastors and ministers were transformed, revived and refined at the altars every night. People saved even walking in off the streets. Sometimes when police would pick up people on the streets they brought them to the revival because they knew people were genuinely being changed by the power of God. Millions passed through this remarkable Outpouring of God's Spirit. There are testimonies of ministers throughout the world who were practically shipwrecked in their churches and ministries and they came to the Outpouring of God's Spirit and were set free from religion and freshly anointed and they returned to transformed ministries as they brought back the fire of God.

The Lord impressed on me to schedule time in my calendar to return to the revival and submerge myself in the river of God that was flowing in this place. Lois did not have to be convinced, she was ready. We went back to Brownsville twenty-four times in a period of just a few years. Each time God melted our hearts, perfected us, spoke to us, filled us and gave us a fresh impartation of His Spirit and anointing.

We learned about the "Glory." The Hebrew word for "glory" means "heavy/weighty". Glory means, mind-blowing, weightiness of God's presence. In the Bible, we see people literally/physically blown away, overcome, almost crushed at times as they glimpse the "weightiness of God". The Bible tells us that God's glory is so awesome that even the angels in heaven bow down on the ground before Him. *"And after these things I heard a great voice of much people in heaven, saying, Alleluia; Salvation, and glory, and honour, and power, unto the Lord our God: For true and righteous are his judgments: for he hath judged the great whore, which did corrupt the earth with her fornication, and hath avenged the blood of his servants at her hand. And again they said, Alleluia And her smoke rose up for ever and ever. ⁴ And the four and twenty elders and the four beasts fell down and worshiped God that sat on the throne, saying, Amen; Alleluia"* Revelation 19:1-2, 4.

Paul the Apostle was arrested by the brightness of
the Glory of God and was thrown from his horse. ³
And as he journeyed, he came near Damascus: and
suddenly there shined round about him a light from
heaven: And he fell to the earth and heard a voice
saying unto him, Saul, Saul, why persecutest thou me?
Acts 9:3-4

Pastor Kilpatrick was arrested by the Presence of
the Holy Spirit many times when he would be out
and feeling a heavy weight Presence of God on him
he could not move. He would be slouched over in
his chair for hours. On Father's Day 1995 when the
Revival started Pastor Kilpatrick stated he felt as if
a mighty wind blew through the bottom of his legs
and overtook him and laid him out on the floor four
hours. When he shares this story, he relates his prior
resistance to being "out of control," and being very
cautious because even though he was hungry for God
to move he did not want anything to be out of order,

or might we say out of his control. However, the hunger in his heart for God superseded any fear of something being out of control. One night before a revival in a session of intercessory prayer in the early morning hours he laid the keys of the church on the altar as an act of submission and abandonment to God's will and His workings.

Lois went to the morning conference with Michael Brown. I would drop her off and come back later as I was still walking cautiously and digesting everything from the previous night's service. When I went back to pick Lois up from the morning conference I asked her what he taught on and she said in tears and conviction, "die, die, die." I responded "well I need something a little more encouraging and I'll have to recover from the hard hits from the message last night, just give me time. "Steve Hill preached a tremendously convicting message that even a Christian would take a hard look and examine their life and heart. His message summoned the sinner to the altar and even Christians who were lukewarm and many religious found rededication and the power they were missing in their lives and ministries. Never have I heard anyone with the passion for souls that Steve had.

I know there are critics but if there was anyone who was doubtful and cautious it was me. However, after 24 trips there and a ten-year relationship with Pastor Kilpatrick, six years working together to hold Fire and Glory Crusades I am no longer a doubter because my life and ministry were transformed. I also know Pastor Kilpatrick is a man of the utmost integrity. Any criticism is an attack of the enemy. Azusa street had critics too. All revivals have had critics or I might say many outright lies designed to undermine the holy working of the Holy Spirit. There were critics who deny the resurrection of Jesus as being a fact however the Truth prevails in the lives of those who have been transformed by its power. My best argument on that subject is found in the words of the songwriter who penned the anointed words, He Lives, he Lives, He Lives, you ask me how I know He lives, He lives within my heart."

Each trip we made to Pensacola to the Brownsville Revival we bought as many tapes and books we could possibly afford and more. Today those revival resources line the bookcases in our home and office and garage and provide the spiritual fuel we need to maintain our anointing and fire of God flowing in our lives. We make it a point to invite hungry God-seekers to our home and show them the powerful services with the manifestation of the power and Presence of God. The anointing is so strong on these videos people have been slain in the Spirit on our living room carpet. When they get up they want to come back for more. Thank God, He doesn't limit the supply but you can have as much as you are hungry for.

Our new hunger for MORE of Him led us to Toronto, Smithtown, Kansas City. Each one of these places had outpourings of the Holy Spirit each having a different emphasis. God doesn't do imitations He does originals. That's important to remember as you pray for Revival in your church and city.

God led us to take several people to the Revival in Brownsville. We took several ministers and they were forever grateful of what they experienced and took back home with them to their churches.

We also partnered with Rev. Rafael Calderon who also had the same experience of revival. His church on N27th St in Camden NJ was completely transformed by the Fire of His Spirit and remains today a church that has the Spirit of Revival. We brought revival messages to churches and went to Caracas, Venezuela together where we had a major crusade. We ministered in several churches in our district bringing the message of the fire of God and imparting hunger for revival.

If you would ask me to define revival in one sentence I would say: REVIVAL IS A RENEWED RELATIONSHIP WITH JESUS CHRIST! Revival is all about Jesus, more of Him, Less of me and MORE OF HIM.

CHAPTER 14

GOD'S DETAIL BROOMS TO REFINE AND SWEEP US CLEAN

"I believe God's ministers are to be flames of fire. Nothing less than flames. Nothing less than mighty instruments, with burning messages, with hearts full of love. They must have a depth of consecration, that God has taken full charge of the body, and it exists only that it may manifest the Glory of God." Smith Wigglesworth

The Lord burned three major principles into my heart. Refinement through repentance, humility, and holiness, Re-firing or Renovation by the Holy Spirit through Intimacy and Worship and Redirection in my ministry.

God was calling us to Deeper depths and higher heights. God was saying 95 per cent holiness is not enough. Michael Brown was delivering a strong message about Dying to self and living for Him at a new level of commitment. As I mentioned earlier I would drop Lois off for the morning conference with Dr. Michael Brown. Die, Die, Die, seemed like an invitation to an execution and I wasn't ready for it. However, one morning I went. I knew I had to face the truth sooner or later that there was indeed more and I needed to do my part to press into the depths of God even if it meant a change in my own life.

I remember being in the service and as Dr. Brown preached, the Word of God riveted through me bringing conviction to a closer walk with the Lord. The Lord showed me I was living below my potential as a minister of the Gospel and He had so much more to my life and ministry if I was willing to make a commitment that superseded my desires and wants and not "pick and choose" but really mean it when I said,

"Thy will be done." During more than one hundred Revival services filled with the fire of God and the anointing of the Holy Spirit, God used many different "Brooms" to sweep us clean and refine us. Every time we thought God was done He brought out another broom. It was like going into a new season and we thought He was done then out came another broom, one for Fall, Winter, Spring and Summer. "Consider what you are missing if you love Jesus with only half a heart." (Basilea Schlink)

Just imagine what we could do in many years of service –if we paid the price and pressed into the depths of God without reservation and continued to fuel the fire of God in our hearts. ***"Wherefore I put thee in remembrance that thou stir up the gift of God, which is in thee by the putting on of my hands."*** 2 Timothy 1:6

"Not slothful in business; fervent in spirit; serving the Lord." Romans 12:11

"And let us not be weary in well doing: for in due season we shall reap if we faint not." Galatians 6:9

As Steve Hill said repeatedly in his messages: "Is the life you're living for worth Christ dying for?"

Corrie Ten-Boom said, "Beware of the barrenness of a busy life."

GOD'S BROOM OF REPENTANCE

"There are three persons living in each of us: the one we think we are, the one other people think we are, and the one God knows we are."
Leonard Ravenhill

After being subjected to the searchlight of the Holy Spirit in the fire of Revival repentance was something we did frequently as we realized that even the "little things" bring our lives out of alignment with God's good pleasure and favor towards our lives. *"If we confess our sins, he is faithful and just to forgive us*

our sins, and to cleanse us from all unrighteousness."
I John 1:9

Repentance… refreshing… return…. Restoration. Repentance opens the portals of refreshing and blessing on our lives. God is looking for yielded vessels, instruments suited for His use. They must be emptied of selfish ambition and dead to religious or self-serving agendas that bring more glory to man than to God. God is looking for people who will be willing to go anywhere and do anything that will win souls and bring glory to Him. God was emptying me of my own desires and agenda and I was brought to a place of repentance so that I could adequately answer God's call on my life. I was not living in sin, I was saved but it was the little things that God was convicting us of.

God convicted me of making decisions on my own and being sure to have His will. I repented of my stubbornness in accepting God's call to minister to Spanish-speaking people. I wasted time arguing with God when all along God knew that if I would trust Him and move out in faith He planned to give me the ability to speak Spanish. I thank God, He dealt with me in mercy.

God showed us the importance of keeping a short account with Him and looking over our lives each day and repenting of unforgiveness, and bad attitudes, lack of praise and complaining. We were much more careful now to not offend the Holy Spirit by lacking the Christian character that pleases Him.

God dealt with both Lois and me about getting rid of extra baggage that hindered our walk. We keep a regular practice of self-examination and repentance to assure our hearts are clean before the Lord.

Thank God for the blood of Jesus and God's forgiveness.

GOD'S BROOM OF HUMILITY – NEW LEVEL OF SENSITIVITY

But he giveth more grace. Wherefore he saith, God resisteth the proud, but giveth grace unto the humble. James 4:6

God told me to GIVE HIM THE GLORY. Don't take it for yourself. When Lois and I would leave the service, we would immediately give all the compliments and praise that the people showered on us, we would give it all to Him.

As we sought the Lord it seemed He was requiring a deeper commitment to living a holy life insomuch as the little things were important as well as humbling ourselves to receive. Many times, we find the power of God poured out powerfully and extravagantly in humble places. In the Azusa Outpouring, we find God's power being poured out in an abandoned Methodist church used as a horse stable and warehouse. In the early nineteenth century, His power was poured out in the primitive woods of Kentucky. In the eighteenth century God moved mightily and miraculously in a damaged cannon factory spreading toward the open fields of England. Even going all the way back to the sixteenth century, it was a dilapidated chapel in Wittenberg that hosted the Word and the Spirit's moving.

The secret here was, humble people were stepping out of the way to make room for the Holy Spirit. The Lord told me to stay humble in mind, spirit and attitude and not to exalt my ideas or methods above His. I would quickly learn that no matter how many degrees or techniques or abilities that I had for getting the job done that I was still an earthen vessel and my purpose was to show off the King of Glory residing in me and bring praise and glory and honor to Him who is worthy to be praised. Paul refers to us as earthen vessels carrying the power of God. When God comes in His power like we saw Him come in the Brownsville Revival it is our responsibility to give it away and not keep it all for ourselves.

Lois and I enjoyed bringing people who were hungry to the revival and seeing them get filled up and renewed. We saw pastors refreshed and renewed and able to return to their ministries and churches with a new vision and fresh power to impart to their churches. We visited some of those churches after we returned to NJ and we were encouraged to see these churches all lit up with a fresh hunger and fervency to seek the Lord. The worship and atmosphere were lit up with the Presence of God and people were acting like they were enjoying church whereas before they were apathetic and lukewarm.

Sometimes pride keeps people from recognizing they need revival.

"A genuine revival, where the transformation of life is demonstrated through confession and acts of reconciliation, is not possible without humility, and this level of humility is the key to any revival."
Andrew Murray

GOD'S BROOM OF HOLINESS

"The early church was married to poverty, prisons, and persecutions. Today, the church is married to prosperity, personality, and popularity." Leonard Ravenhill

If we are to understand the importance of holiness we need to have a clear understanding of what it is and what it is not. It seems to be a common practice among Pentecostals through the span of time to create rules and regulations concerning holiness rather than adhere strictly to the Biblical context. I think God had more in mind then dressing in a certain uniform and having a certain hairdo when He emphasizes the importance of holiness in the Word of God. Any organization can require a uniform for membership but God's body of believers throughout the world consist of millions of people from diverse cultures.

I would like to suggest that there would be less confusion and disunity on the subject if we understood that culture changes but doctrine never changes. Let me explain: The doctrines of the Bible one such as Salvation, for example, does not change throughout the world. Jesus saves through the blood He shed on Calvary's cross. We are saved when we recognize we are sinners and repent and become new creatures. That message does not change whether you're in Africa or Asia, Europe or the USA. However, culture does change; that means, styles, clothes, trends etc. all change continent to continent, people groups to people groups. However, we need to be very careful about our conduct and how we dress as we are giving testimony continually and showcasing the glory of God.

As a pastor, you may have a code of dress for your worship team or others participating in ministry and I do too. But I let them know this is a standard of the ministry and not a doctrine of salvation as some preach it. God has called us to preach Christ. We know God has commanded holiness and that we will not see Him without it.

When we returned to our home after each trip to the Outpouring in Florida the Holy Spirit dealt with us on different levels. I remember on our first trip when we came home the Lord said to "clean out the DVD and video cabinet under the TV. My response was "But Lord we don't look at bad movies." The Lord said, "Throw out even ones that may have just one word because that one word can hurt your anointing." We quickly obeyed and threw out even movies that were the least bit questionable not only by word but by theme or even implication. What we had tasted, seen, felt, and experienced in the Outpouring of the Holy Spirit was worth giving anything up for. We wanted to sustain the Wonderful Presence of God that had filled us and made us even hungrier for more of Him. We were careful examining our hearts and lives to keep from offending His Precious Holy Spirit. That became a priority in our spiritual maintenance every day. Holiness is all about pleasing Him. We must be careful not to relegate it to a mere completion of a list of do's and don'ts.

It was important to us now to keep the atmosphere in our home holy. That would mean putting a check on conversations, relationships, and attitudes. The fruit of a changed mind is a sanctified life.

God required sanctification of the people in Israel.

"And the Lord said unto Moses, Go unto the people, and sanctify them today and tomorrow, and let them wash their clothes, And be ready against the third day: for the third day the Lord will come down in the sight of all the people upon mount Sinai." Exodus 19:10-11

Prior to the visible manifestation of the glory of God on Mount Sinai, they were to sanctify themselves and prepare to be in the Presence of a holy God. We cannot present ourselves before the Lord with our lives in disorder. This was the tragedy in the case of Nadab and Abihu. They had taken part in the consecration of the priests. They saw the shekinah, the glory of God, descending on the tabernacle and fire coming out from the Presence of God to consume the offering, a symbol of surrender and consecration. *And Aaron lifted up his hand toward the people, and blessed them, and came down from the offering of the sin offering, and the burnt offering, and peace offerings.*

And Moses and Aaron went into the tabernacle of the congregation, and came out, and blessed the people: and the glory of the Lord appeared unto all the people.

And there came a fire out from before the Lord and consumed upon the altar the burnt-offering and the fat: which when all the people saw, they shouted, and fell on their faces.

But the next day they attempted to offer the incense to God with their lives in disorder, using unauthorized fire that God had not sent, and they were consumed by God's wrath. *And Nadab and Abihu, the sons of Aaron, took either of them his censer, and put fire therein, and put incense thereon, and offered strange fire before the Lord, which he commanded them not.And there went out fire from the Lord and devoured them, and they died before the Lord. Then Moses said unto Aaron, This is it that the Lord spake, saying, I will be sanctified in them that come nigh me, and before all the people I will be glorified. And Aaron held his peace.* Leviticus 10:1-3

They did not acknowledge His glory or prepare to meet Him in the holiness that He demands of His people. They were not able to distinguish between what was holy and what was worldy. Maybe they considered God as a means of fulfilling their own ambitions or desires. It seems we have the same problem in the church today. Christians need to draw a clear line between the world the flesh and the devil and the holiness of God

We understand the Bronze Altar where the animals were killed as the law prescribed was a place of worship and death but also representing the cross of Jesus Christ. We are saved by believing in Christ who was crucified and resurrected from the dead. However, we must understand the message of the cross of Christ calls to us every day as we are instructed in Luke 9:23 ***"If anyone would come after me, he must deny himself and take up his cross daily and follow me."***

After the outpouring of the Holy Spirit afresh and anew I was more convicted about little things that could offend the Holy Spirit. I also had a deeper commitment to seeing the glory and Presence of God in our lives and realized that depth of commitment would cost us everything. God was calling me to lay aside every weight and any excess baggage that would slow me up in seeing the fulfillment of God's will in my life. I knew that meant not just laying aside known sin, but laying aside anything that interfered with what the Holy Spirit was doing and where He was leading me. There was no room for bargaining with God and I had to be prepared to say no to my will, intellect, and emotions when they were contrary to God's will.

We realized that when we turned over to God all that we loved – our plans, our time, our family, our work-everything- we turned the key that unlocks the door to a mighty visitation of God's Spirit in our lives, churches, and ministries. The American Gospel has conjured up too many shortcuts. We must consider the ancient paths if we want to get on the road to a visitation of God's Spirit.

My motivations, my thoughts, my ambitions, my de-sires my innermost being – God wants it all.

After tasting of the Glory and Presence of God I was willing to seek Him more fervently to have His Abiding Presence in my life. After seeing God move in such a powerful way I knew I could never go back to the status quo of religious ways but keep seeking for more of Him. That search meant all carnal ways would have to cease and we would daily be conscious of the Holy Spirit's spotlight upon my ways and words and my goal was to please Him.

I believe God is waiting for the modern church to repent of worldliness and carnal ways and remove the stumbling blocks of religion and apathy and luke-warmness so that God can send a fresh outpouring of His Spirit in our lives and in our churches. When we look at the revivalists of years past it should stir the most worldly, apathetic person and church to re-pent, be refreshed, return and be restored.

George Whitefield was red hot for the Lord. Between the ages of twenty to fifty-six, he delivered about 30,000 sermons. He preached about 40-60 hours a week. Without microphones or fancy sound systems and digital electronics, he ministered to crowds of up to 40,000. He preached in every town in England, Scotland, and Wales and Ireland as well during 34 years of his ministry. He sailed the Atlantic seven times and won thousands to the Lord in northern and south America. All of this using eighteenth-century means of transportation.

CHAPTER 15

RENOVATED IN THE FIRE OF REVIVAL

PRAYER

"After they prayed, the place where they were meeting was shaken. And they were all filled with the Holy Spirit and spoke the word of God boldly. Acts 4:31

P rayer is powerful and needs a place of pre-eminence in our lives. Before the revival, my prayer life was boring and religious lacking life and power. I followed a list of needs and the prayer time was spent presenting those needs. I thought I was being Biblical and obedient. However, after revival and fresh impartation of the Holy Spirit, my prayer life was quickened. It became more about relationship and communion and fellowship with the Holy Spirit rather than going through a laundry list of needs. Now I was motivated by my renewed love for Jesus and my desire to want to spend time with Him rather than going thru some sort of religious rhetoric.

There seems to be a high tech, microwave mentality in the modern church today. We want everything quickly and the word "wait" is like a foreign language. Our world around us even in the church is built around being quick, and to the point that even our services we promise and advertise "we'll have you out by 12 noon." What if God has another plan? Maybe He is going to move mightily at 12:05. We jam everything into a time segment and God help us if we must "wait."

This is one of the problems in prayer. We must wait on God and take our time in His Presence and not be in a hurry. Of course, I recognize there are times we need to shoot up to heaven a quick prayer but we should also have a time when we "wait" on God.

I'm ever so thankful God changed my prayer life even though I still pray in shorter intervals I look forward to giving God some time when I'm not rushed by the clock or my own agenda or schedule.

Prayer enables me to build a personal relationship as I commune with my Savior and I talk to the Lover of my Soul, my Jesus. God, Himself is the answer to my prayers.

I learned the importance of persevering prayer. That means not caving in and giving up. If we rend our hearts God will rend heaven. Many parts of China are experiencing great revival. The Chinese Christians have sought the Lord fervently in past decades. They've labored, toiled and sown.

The prayers of one righteous man impacted a nation when Elijah who James 5:17 says was "a man just like us," He took hold of God and prayed and would not let go asking God earnestly that it would not rain, and it did not rain for three and a half years." The prayers of one righteous man literally impacted the whole nation.

The Lord thru the renewal and revival in my life gave me more fervor and faith for prayer. Listening to hundreds of life changing testimonies of people who were transformed in the Revival gave me a desire to want to seek the Lord and believe for mighty miracles in our lives and ministry. I would learn from the Holy Spirit that my plans and agenda would have to be modified to make room for an adequate prayer life.

Prayer takes time but it is the key to having a move of God in your life or church. It is easier to pick a promise and stand upon it. But that's not what God has in mind. It's all about relationship. God's purpose is that we have fellowship with Him The men and women of God who have made an impact on the world have all been, without exception constant and persist in prayer.

I found I needed to silence all the voices that tempted me to give up on my spiritual search. When God began to move in my life in a way I had not seen before I knew it was truly worth it to cultivate the discipline of prayer. The peace of God always accompanied my times in prayer.

I began to pray God would break my heart with the things that broke His heart. After praying for my neighbors to be saved God has now opened doors and two have gotten saved and there are some others I'm waiting for that opportune moment and in the meantime developing a friendship with them. God answers prayer. There is power in prayer.

Before Pentecost, the disciples were ordered to wait. *"Stay in the city of Jerusalem until you have been clothed with power from on high."* Luke 24:49

Before hearing God's voice from the cloud of glory,

Moses had to wait on the mountain.

If we want to see the glory of God like we say we do then we need to wait in His Presence.

Even after the Lord has lit the fire of the Holy Spirit in our hearts, we must keep the flame alive.

And the fire upon the altar shall be burning in it; it shall not be put out: and the priest shall burn wood on it every morning, and lay the burnt offering in order upon it, and he shall burn thereon the fat of the peace offerings.

The fire shall ever be burning upon the altar; it shall never go out. Leviticus 6:12-13

In the tabernacle, a priest had the daily responsibility of looking after the fire. He had to take away the ashes and add more wood each morning. Even on cold winter mornings he had to hunt down the wood, load it up on his shoulders and take it to the altar and put it on the fire. Our prayer lives help fan the flame of revival and we need to take seriously God's command to pray. It takes discipline and dedication but it is necessary to stoke the flames of friendship, faithfulness, and companionship on a daily basis.

All fires tend to go out if they are not maintained. Relationships can deteriorate if we don't tend to them. We know that is true in the marital relationship when the flame of love is not fanned and nurtured. Our relationship with God is the same way. We must "Draw near to Him." God spoke to my heart clearly about prayer after revival. The Holy Spirit said to me "He does not work on automatic." It's a personal, intimate relationship that requires my personal attention, love, and pursuit after a closer relationship. I fell radically in love with Jesus all over again and it's my job to work at guarding that relationship through the discipline of prayer.

I really learned the importance of the discipline of the power of prayer and knowing God's voice after I experienced a Jezebel experience in Guatemala with one of my leaders. I was mentoring a discipline in this person to take on more and more responsibility in the mission ministry. She was a tremendous worker who did more than anyone as far as producing and accomplishing assignments.

However, I learned that the sneaky spirit of sabotage was at work and it had to be stopped. I didn't realize there was a spirit at work seeking to derail my ministry and then imitate it in launching her own ministry. It wasn't until someone God uses in intercession began to give me the spiritual evidence that this individual was operating in the spirit of Jezebel and I must stop it.

The prayer warrior who told me about the spirit of sabotage also told me where she learned about it: Cindy Trimm's book The Rules of Engagement. She discusses the spirit of sabotage on pages 245-246:

«*The Spirit of Sabotage operates as strong demonic influences* that drive people to abort the progress and success of divinely ordained projects, purposes, relationships, organization, self, potential, and destinies. It stirs up jealousy, resentment, and suspicion, and is often vindictive toward the person who detects its presence. Sabotage can make you both victim and perpetrator so that even when you pronounce judgment on others you both expose and pronounce judgment upon yourself.

«This spirit is so skillful it will use you as a pawn and a puppet on a string, prohibiting you from detecting its hand upon you and the strings that manipulate you. Working with familiar spirits, who act as their reconnaissance, informing them of breaks in hedges of protection, strengths, weaknesses and proclivities of both the perpetrator and victim, its plan is a well-thought-out plan.

«I have discovered that many agents used are not only those with malicious intent but also those who sincerely love us and want what›s best for us. Consider the incident Matthew records In Matthew 16:21-23, where Peter unwittingly was being used in an attempt to sabotage the mission of Jesus. Jesus decisively identified the spirit controlling Peter›s thoughts and immediately *aborted its activities.*

«Remember as you examine the activities of this spirit that you will discover that you are both victim and perpetrator. When the Lord gives you victory over this spirit, you will notice that a veil will be lifted, and scales of deception will fall from your spiritual eyes. Everything that you thought was real will crumble before you and evaporate like a mirage. The truth will prevail and set you free from anything built upon fabrications, lies, falsehood and untruths.»

I became so discouraged I said to the Lord, "I'm finished." The Lord responded: "You will not quit and leave Guatemala in defeat but the day you leave will be in great victory." So obviously I didn't quit. God worked it all out for His glory. The process was not easy because Jezebel created a powerful defense consisting of all the things she had done for me. But God brought her down and stopped her from prospering in what she was seeking to accomplish. God defended my ministry and I'm still carrying on the work He called me to do in Guatemala.

Through this experience, God taught me a new depth and discernment in prayer I believe all ministers need. He also taught me to listen to my intercessors who God has placed by me for my protection. I appreciate the ministry of intercession and prophecy now more than ever.

My goal after revival is to walk in daily fellowship with the Holy Spirit, maintain my spiritual fervor and never get caught up in the spokes of a religious routine. Prayer is not a monolog but a majestic dialogue so I needed to learn more about hearing the voice of God. One day I was rattling off a bunch of religious prayers and the Lord told me to "Be still, and hear His voice." Now I pray, "Lord, plunge me into your river keep me there I want to hear you and depend on you."

WORSHIP & INTIMACY

**"If there is no laughter, Jesus has gone somewhere else.
If there is no joy and freedom,
it is not a church: it is simply a crowd of melancholy
people basking in a religious neurosis.
If there is no celebration, there is no real worship."**
Steve Brown

One of the most powerful truths I experienced in the revival was a new understanding of the importance of the Presence of God. The first night when Lindell Cooley started to sing and worship it was very different than church services I had been in. I felt something that I had never experienced in all the years I had ministered or had been attending services. I felt the Presence of God like I had never felt it before.

His Presence riveted through my being. I was completely overtaken by His Presence. I had been filled with the Holy Spirit for 25 years and spoke in tongues, but this was different. His Presence permeated every fiber of my being. My stomach began to do somersaults and I was weeping. I said to the Lord, "What is this Father, I'm Pentecostal and speak in tongues but this is more powerful?" The Holy Spirit said to me, "You have learned about my Holy Spirit in books and earned degrees but there is an intimate relationship that doesn't come through books or degrees and if you yield to me I will teach you about it and I will use you to bring it to the churches." From that moment, I dedicated myself to a deeper life in the Spirit and submerging myself in the river of His Presence. My life was never the same after being "arrested," by the Spirit of God. This was also a learning experience and I will share some of the lessons I learned.

I had to get to the place where I was no longer satisfied to read or hear about other people's experiences I had to desperately hunger for my very own encounter with the Holy Spirit. Now there's something in me that drives me in the pursuit of more of God. That kind of hunger takes you beyond the parameters of organized religion, form or ritualistic behavior. That desperate hunger expressed in worship releases the Presence of God.

Worship is the key here. We understand praise, being a celebration. In praise, we thank God for something He has done. I compare **Praise and worship with praise being the engagement and worship the marriage.** The deeper commitment is in the marriage of course. That's where we find intimacy. Worship is expressing love and adoration to God just because He is worthy of the glory and honor. The mission of the worship team in our churches should be to take us into His Presence but many times we fail to complete the journey. When we understand that our goal is intimacy we will have a different attitude about the process.

Worship is an attitude of heart in which the heart bows down before God. Your mind is devoid of all other thoughts other than God. You are not petitioning or needing a healing you are pursuing His Presence because your heart loves Him so much that all you want to do is pour out your love to the Lord. It is a time of love. He pours out His love on us but in worship, we are pouring out our love to Him.

Ruth Heflin said, "When the pattern is right, the glory will fall." **In learning to host the Holy Spirit we find there is a pattern and if we flow in the pattern, no matter what song we sing it'll work. Find the song the Holy Spirit likes and the glory will come into the service.**

When we start worshipping in our services we need to remember we are on a journey and we have a destination. Keep going until the Spirit of worship comes into the meeting and you reach your destination. If the anointing falls on a song keep singing it to reach the top of the mountain. The ministry of praise increases the anointing but worship brings the glory.

Ruth Heflin said, "Praise until worship comes and worship until the glory comes."

Worship should be lavish. We shouldn't hold back anything. We need manifestations of the Presence of God. We know about the omnipresence of God being that God is everywhere. The manifest presence of God is when He manifests and His Presence comes into the atmosphere.

It is the time we sing and dance before Him with all our strength like David danced. God wants His people to clap their hands for joy in His Presence with such power and authority that the devil will cower with his demons to avoid the crippling blows of God's glory.

When we praise Him sacrificially and humbly worship Him prostrating ourselves before Him we will build a glorious sanctuary for His glory.

I won't be satisfied until I'm standing in the Glory. Worship brings you into the bridal chamber from just courting. If you are married you understand the difference between wedding day and the bridal chamber. As a serious worshipper, I have a different understanding now and I don't want to stay in the outer courts and miss out on anything God has for me.

Revival for me meant Renewed Intimacy with Jesus Christ. I learned that God's master plan for church growth is fruitfulness through intimacy. Children will be born when the church returns to intimacy and a fresh encounter with the Holy Spirit. The truth of the matter is people have been doing things for a long, long time in our churches, with very little to show for it. We don't need another method or "How to it, technique, we need SOMEONE. We need God Himself to move, and to take us beyond the limits of our understanding and knowledge and to come and dwell among us. But unfortunately, what happens many times is that we're so busy developing the structure and plans for our services that there is no room for His Presence, for interruptions, even from God Himself. We must invite Him to interrupt us. We must make room for the Holy Spirit.

God changed my goals for my preaching ministry. When I saw what the Presence of God did for me and how He changed pastors and ministries night after night in hundreds of services, I was convinced that the greatest need in the church today is the PRESENCE OF GOD. I watched ministers submit to the awesome Presence of God and watched His Presence heal areas in lives that were falling apart, men and women of God dried up and tired of working hard and seeing nothing, get transformed with fresh encounters with the Holy Spirit. I saw their faces lit up as they went from being hopeless to now being recharged with the power of God and were ready to bring the Presence of God back to their ministries and churches.

After being renovated in the fire of revival I had a burning desire to take His Presence to the churches where I ministered. My goal was no longer to just have a beautiful sermon but to minister from the heart of God and see manifestations of His Presence in my services. My preparation time for ministry now became a passionate pursuit for His Presence to saturate me so I could take it to the churches.

The Presence of God has changed my life and my ministry forever. It is my passion now to impart a hunger for God's Presence wherever I go and be that vessel so yielded and saturated by the fire of God that others will want His Presence also. The more I soak in His Presence the more anointing I have when I minister. It was a miracle how God rescued my ministry and put life and fruitfulness in it after over 25 years.

The last 23 years have been the most exciting, fruitful and Presence filled times of my ministry. Before revival, I was just going thru the mechanics of religious ideas on how to have a successful ministry but now I was operating more by the power of the Holy Spirit who was enabling me with a fire anointing every time I ministered. It is such a joy and privilege now to go to a church and talk about being hungry for God's Presence and at the altar call seeing people crying out to God for more of His Presence.

When people have a fresh encounter with the Holy Spirit their faces light up and they testify later that they never felt the Presence of God like they felt Him that day. I give all the glory and honor and praise to God for bringing me into this wonderful season with a fresh and powerful anointing to do His work not in my strength or ability but by His power. *"Then he answered and spake unto me, saying, This is the word of the Lord* unto Zerubbabel, saying, Not by might, nor by power, but by my spirit, *saith the Lord* of hosts." Zechariah 4:6

CHAPTER 16

REDIRECTION –NEW MANDATE

But none of these things move me, neither count I my life dear unto myself so that I might finish my course with joy, and the ministry, which I have received of the Lord Jesus, to testify the gospel of the grace of God. Acts 20:24

FANNING THE FLAME OF REVIVAL This was the new theme for our ministry. *"The fire shall ever be burning upon the altar; it shall never go out."* Leviticus 6:13

FANNING THE FLAME OF REVIVAL PROJECT IN USA

During the first 10 years after we were transformed in the Brownsville Revival, God opened the door to host Crusades where I would speak on Sunday and Wednesday and I would have either John Kilpatrick or Lindell Cooley or the Grays who were anointed revivalists minister on Monday and Tuesday. I did two of these crusades a year up until 2009. God wonderfully and powerfully came down. Churches were set ablaze with a new fervency and zeal with a renewed vision for revival. Pastor Kilpatrick said I was like a revival daughter and that was evidenced by the messenger that I became heralding the message of revival. The years during my Fanning The Flame of Revival Project were very exciting times where we saw God do many miracles of renovating and bringing pastors and congregations into a fresh encounter with the Holy Spirit.

ACCEPTING THE MANDATE FOR MISSIONS

In 1996 God began to put on my heart the word that Pastor Moses Moran spoke to me years ago: "You are our missionary. God sent you here to Chamelco." After a revival in 1997, God gave me the mandate and the vision. The mandate was necessary for me to move forward. A ministry cannot be successful on simply the words of a man there must be a mandate, a command from God. When a man or woman of God receives a mandate from God through thick and thin, trials and suffering and disillusionments and setbacks they will keep going and they will not quit. After the Holy Spirit filled me with a fresh fire and put the message of revival on my heart the Lord brought back to my mind again the words of Pastor Moses Moran "You are our missionary. God sent you here to Chamelco." The Lord told me He had equipped me now to take on this mandate and I would Fan the Fame of Revival in Guatemala through Mission work. The Lord gave me the Vision to accomplish the Mandate.

THE VISION

Change The Destiny of a Child, A Church, A Community

1. **Change The Destiny of a Child** would be accomplished through helping them build an elementary school that Pastor Moses had a dream to do for many years.

2. **Change the Destiny of a Church** would be done through Fanning the Flame of Revival and seeing the supernatural growth that would follow.

3. **Taking Groups to Guatemala to do Short-Term Mission Trips**. Support for projects would be supplied partially through the

group trips. In addition, the groups would be mentored, disciplined and equipped in doing mission work. During 20 years of taking 100's of people many have been transformed, called and received fresh encounters with the Holy Spirit. Since the mission work is in a revival charged atmosphere and the crusade services are powerful the Mission Team receives a fresh touch of God upon their lives with renewed commitment to work in their local church. Others have been called to various ministries and are serving in different areas of ministry. Since we are a bilingual ministry we are ministering to Americans who also help compose the mission team. We presently have a Teacher-Evangelist who is doing bilingual ministry and served on my staff for more than 5 years, Rev. Santos Rivera a minister of the Gospel for many years who expanded his borders of ministry and is now doing the same apostolic model of our ministry in the Dominican Republic. He is seeing miracles in his ministry and is also reproducing disciples from his ministry. I thank God, our ministry is reproducing ministers who are carrying the vision of Fanning the Flame of Revival.

4. **Evangelistic Crusades** – In every Crusade we saw the Fire and Glory of God. After I returned from the revival in Florida Pastor Moses asked me what had happened because he saw a change in me. I told him my story of how God had mightily transformed me and given me a passion for His Presence. I gave him a book to read by Tommy Tenney, The God Chasers and I showed him some videos of the services with the Manifest Presence of God coming down and blessing the church. He said to me, "I want this."

I began to emphasize the importance of worship in the services and the need for a worship team. Through prayer, we were able to realize that dream and finally, in the next several crusades, we had three worship teams. There was one worship team in standby mode so they could take over when the others "fell out in the Spirit." Unexpectedly the church received a keyboard mailed from the United States with no name. We all praised God for the much-needed instrument to complete the worship teams' needs. Once the worship team was in full action we began to see the moving of the Holy Spirit and revival intensify in every service.

He began to teach the church in detail the Book of Acts. Pastor Moses and his wife Marina and I and Lois made a great team with Pastor Moses being the teacher and me the evangelist tending to the revival. I would "Fan the Flame of Revival," during the crusades and Pastor Moses would teach, disciple and oversee the church and school on a daily basis. He was an amazing teacher and a man with much perseverance and determination to keep pressing on to the goal despite trials and tribulations.

After Revival started in 2001 we saw the salvation of multitudes of people. In six months, we baptized and received as members of the church 120 people indicating the rapid growth that Revival had brought. When I started with this church before all the crusades we had less than 100 in attendance and after revival over 400. In our crusade services, it was common to see worship to last for 2 hours and even before anyone preached people come running to the altar to get saved and delivered.

There have been notable miracles such as:

Little girl healed of appendicitis- She was taken to a doctor with pain and told she needed an operation for appendicitis and she asked to go home and pray and God answered prayer and healed her. Not only did God heal her but saved her entire family.

The serious spinal injury healed – A man came into crusade service in a wheelchair with his wife. They came to the altar and were prayed for and after prayer, the man was able to get up out of the wheelchair, and walk to the back of the church and back up front with help.

The second night he came back again with his wife but walking with only a cane. The third night he returned and he didn't have even the cane. He was totally healed and shouting the victory. His wife then surrendered her life to the Lord and got saved. She had seen the Presence of God in action and became a believer.

A blind man healed- one eye was without sight and God healed him.

Cancer healed- several women were healed of breast cancer.

There have been innumerable healings that could compose another writing.

5. **Street Ministry** – The street ministry has been a very important part of all our Mission Trips as it is a means of preaching the Gospel, distributing tracts and inviting people to the nightly crusades. One young man came into a service one night and he had a camera. He came to me after the service. I remembered him being at the altar and I had prayed with him to receive Jesus as his Savior and Lord. He told me he wanted to apologize because he came into the service with the intention of photographing and writing negative reports to give to local newspapers.

However, he said I have nothing but good things to say having felt the Presence of God in this place. I want to dedicate my photography gift to your ministry when you are here doing the crusades.

6. **Radio Program** –We saw the power of God at the radio station in Chamelco when revival first started. We brought the Mission Team to the radio program and invited the people who were listening to come to the station for prayer. After the program, the front was filled with people waiting to get inside for prayer. God manifested His power with signs and wonders. We saw healings of deaf ears, babies healed, and many others.

7. **Special Projects Planting churches** – God enabled us to help with several missions being constructed: including helping mother church buying land, putting up foundational structures and putting down flooring, and helping con-

tribute to pastor's support through offerings.

We completed a church on the road between Coban and Chamelco and gave it the name Presence Church in 2015. That work is independent of the work in Chamelco now.

Building or Remodeling of Widows' houses – There were 8 houses either built or remodeled where widows were living in complete poverty. We blessed the parsonage with a renovation and modern appliances also.

Scholarships for Ministers- In the desire to want to see more ministers committed to the work of the Lord we helped several by granting them scholarships to attend Bible Institute. We have several of them Pastoring in El Salvador, Honduras and other parts of Guatemala. They too are carrying the message to Fan the Flame of Revival.

Benevolence Ministry –

Widow Care – We supply bags of food for widows and needy. On our Mission Trips, the team participates in bagging the food and preparing the bags for distribution

Hospitals and Old Age Homes – providing bags of resources and supplies for hospitals and special services clinics and special Evangelistic Services at Nursing homes and supplies according to need.

Extreme needs – funerals, medical needs, clinic visits, operations

8 **Medical Clinics –** We have had several successful medical clinics in Chamelco. God was glorified in healing people even during the Doctor's examination. In one of our medical clinics we attended to approximately 600 people in three days. God was truly glorified.

A lady came one day to be treated at the clinic and after the Dr. saw her, we prayed for her. Before we prayed we noticed she had a Mayan necklace around her neck. We told her that her pagan gods could not do what God could do for her but she needed to give her heart to Jesus. She was greatly touched by the Spirit of God. We told her to take off her necklace in an action to renounce those false gods and she took off the necklace and received Jesus as her Savior and when she threw it down on the floor the necklace pulverized before everyone's eyes. It was now powder on the floor because God is Greater and He showed up and that lady will never be the same.

CHAPTER 17

VISION EXPANDS

"The opportunity of a lifetime must be seized in the lifetime of the opportunity."

Leonard Ravenhill

My vision for Guatemala missions has expanded now. For the past year, I have been partnering with a pastor in Petapa, Villa Hermosa Guatemala. His name is Hector Barillas. The name of his church is Cristo Te Ama. He was recommended to me for my help by Rev. Monterosso the Superintendent of the Assemblies of God in Guatemala. My present vision is to continue with the same apostolic vision but to expand to the City of Guatemala as well as include the region of Alta Vera Paz where I was working for almost 20 years.

Holly Noe Ministries will focus on the following projects and more as the Lord indicates in expanding the Vision.

1. Helping them to complete the Temple they need because of the tremendous growth they are experiencing. Pastor Barillas loves the Presence of God.

2. We are promoting the vision to Fan the Flame of Revival in his section where he is the presbyter.

3. Involve the local church to participate with me in becoming part of our Mission Team as we go to other places in the country ministering and doing mission work. This teaches the people to not only receive from the missionary but become participants themselves in mission work outside of their area.

4. I am also working with the Superintendent to help poor pastors who have no outside help.

5. Planting new missions

6. Continuance of all our benevolence ministries: widows, hospitals. Nursing homes

"For I was an hungred, and ye gave me meat: I was thirsty, and ye gave me drink: I was a stranger, and ye took me in:

Naked, and ye clothed me: I was sick, and ye visited me: I was in prison, and ye came unto me.

Then shall the righteous answer him, saying, Lord, when saw we thee an hungred, and fed thee? or thirsty, and gave thee drink?

When saw we thee a stranger, and took thee in? or naked, and clothed thee?

Or when saw we thee sick, or in prison, and came unto thee?

And the King shall answer and say unto them, Verily I say unto you, Inasmuch as ye have done it unto one of the least of these my brethren, ye have done it unto me." Matthew 25:35-40

7. Scholarships for potential ministers

8. Fire and Glory Crusades – Thank God for the miracles in the crusades. One lady came for prayer in our crusade asking to be able to give birth. When I returned for the next crusade she came to me with a beautiful baby in her hands. After more than 15 years she and her husband finally had a baby. Blind eyes were healed in the hospital and there were miracles of deliverance and restoration. We also saw deaf ears opened. To God be the glory.

9. HIS PRESENCE FOR EVERYONE, AND HIS PRESENCE EVERYWHERE. I am committed to getting out the message about

the need for the Presence of God so that we can return to being like our model church in the Book of Acts.

We need to go from being a program oriented church to a Presence oriented church.

Until Jesus comes – May I continue to be a vessel where the Presence of God can dwell and I can be privileged to carry that Revival Anointing to impart it to others.

"Lord, bend me. Bend the church and save the world." -- Evan Roberts

WHAT NOW LORD, MY LIFE IS WRECKED FOR THE ORDINARY! NOTHING BUT THE SUPERNATURAL WILL SATISFY. THANK YOU, LORD, FOR A LIFE OF MIRACLES. I'M READY FOR MORE

To God Be The Glory For A Life of Miracles And a Supernatural Journey

ABOUT MY ASSOCIATE

Rev. Lois W. Dietrich

Lois has been Associate for Holly Noe Ministries for 30 years, She is a Licensed Minister with the Assemblies of God. She had a very successful career as an elementary school teacher. She received her BS degree at Cedar Crest College. Lois assists in several different areas of Rev. Noe's personal and ministerial life. She ministers at the altar in the services where her warm and affectionate personality and God's anointing is evident. She is loved and admired by all.

She has travelled together with Holly to 15 different countries.

INFORMATION ABOUT HOLLY NOE MINISTRIES

Holly Noe Ministries is available for the following types of ministries:

1. Fire and Glory Crusades
2. Special services
3. Teach missions
4. Special mission services
5. Mission trips to help support the field of labor where they are working.

The focus of these trips is to teach, impart, disciple, and encourage the group to find their place in the Kingdom of God. They will participate in the following ministries; benevolence, outside services, school activities, crusades, helping plant missions and churches, and much more.

CONTACT INFORMATION
Office 732-252-8502 Cell Phone 732-239-3656
Website www.fanningtheflame.org
www.Facebook.com Holly Noe Ministries or
Holly Noe

A LIFE OF MIRACLES
MY SUPERNATURAL JOURNEY

D r. Holly L. Noe will take you on a miraculous journey that begins in her childhood with a demonic possession that led her on a path to despair, depression and bondage. Without God her prognosis was hopeless. However, the Supernatural miracle working God had a call on her life that brought her through deliverance and transformation. The author will captivate you with the stories of her dramatic deliverance.

In Part 2 the road in this journey takes on a new route and direction as she answers the call of God. She then takes you with her to college and then into a traveling ministry where God supernaturally enables her to speak Spanish and then launches her into a ministry to Spanish speaking people.

You will undoubtedly cry and laugh as you follow her to the mission field and read about her very interesting experiences. Finally accompany her to Revival where she experiences a fresh encounter with God's Presence and relates how it happened in a very powerful, personal way. This book will encourage, challenge and convict the reader of the need for an up to date relationship with the Holy Spirit.

ABOUT THE AUTHOR

Rev. Dr. Holly L. Noe is founder and President of Holly Noe Ministries holding a Doctorate in Theology and is ordained with the Assemblies of God. She has traveled throughout the United States and 15 other countries. She has a burden to see the modern church experience the Manifest Presence of God that leads to a fresh encounter with the Holy Spirit. She has a deep love for missions and wants to impart it to others. Dr. Noe imparts hunger for His Presence wherever she ministers as she brings a life changing message to the church.

"Making your book dream come true without robbing you!"

www.deeperlifepress.com

www.findrefuge.tv

79039171R00148

Made in the USA
Columbia, SC
25 October 2017